MFL
AS/A Level

Oxford
Literature
Companions

Der Besuch der alten Dame

FRIEDRICH DÜRRENMATT

Notes and activities:
René Koglbauer and Janine Turner

OXFORD

UNIVERSITY PRESS

Contents

Introduction

What are Oxford Literature Companions?

Oxford Literature Companions for Languages is a series designed to provide you with comprehensive support for popular set texts. You can use the Companion alongside your play, using relevant sections during your studies or using the book as a whole for revision.

Each Companion includes detailed guidance and practical activities on:

- Plot and Structure
- Context
- Characters
- Language
- Themes
- Skills and Practice

How does the book help with exam preparation?

As well as providing guidance on key areas of the play, throughout this book you will also find 'Upgrade' features. These are tips to help with your exam preparation and performance.

In addition, the **Skills and Practice** chapter provides detailed guidance on areas such as how to prepare for the exam, understanding the question, planning your response and hints for what to do (or not do) in the exam. There is also a bank of **Sample questions** and **Sample answers**. The **Sample answers** are marked and include annotations and a summative comment.

How does this book help with terminology?

Throughout the book, key terms are **highlighted** in the text and explained on the same page with the equivalent term in German. There is also a detailed **Glossary** at the end of the book that explains all the relevant literary terms highlighted in this book, with their German translations.

Which edition of this play has been used?

Quotations have been taken from the Diogenes edition of *Der Besuch der alten Dame* (ISBN 9783257230451). Occasionally quotations within this book are accompanied by page references from this edition. Friedrich Dürrenmatt uses the traditional spelling of words such as 'daß'. All spellings in quotations have been kept as in the original text.

How does this book work?

Each book in the Oxford Literature Companions for Languages series follows the same approach and includes the following features:

- **Key quotations** from the play
- **Key terms** explained on the page in English with German translations, linked to a complete glossary at the end of the book
- **Activity boxes** with activities in German to help improve your understanding of the text and your language skills, including:
  - Vocabulary activities
  - Comprehension activities
  - Summary activities
  - Grammar activities
  - Translation activities
  - Extension activities
- **Upgrade** tips to help prepare you for your assessment
- **Useful phrases and vocabulary** in German at the end of each chapter to aid your revision

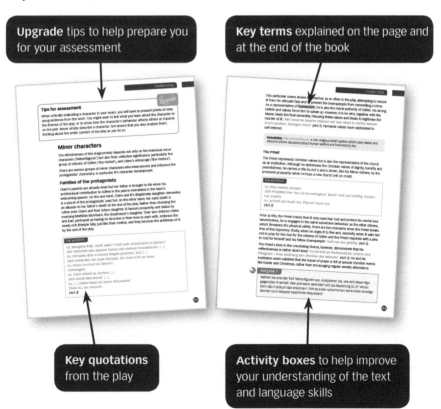

Upgrade tips to help prepare you for your assessment

Key terms explained on the page and at the end of the book

Key quotations from the play

Activity boxes to help improve your understanding of the text and language skills

Plot

Der Besuch der alten Dame tells the story of the elderly billionairess Claire Zachanassian and her mission to demand justice from the people of her small home town, Güllen.

> ### Tips for assessment
>
>
> When reading a play, it is important that you understand the scene descriptions as they give you further information about the setting and the context.

Act 1

Preparations for Claire Zachanassian's visit: *'Glockenton eines Bahnhofs, bevor der Vorhang aufgeht.* [...]'

The play starts at the train station in Güllen. The neglected ('verwahrlost') station represents the run-down and ruined town of Güllen. A sign is visible with the words 'Welcome, Claire' ('Willkommen Kläri') (*Act 1*). Four citizens of Güllen reflect on the fact that a few years ago a number of important trains used to stop there but nowadays hardly any trains stop, and the town is gradually closing down, dragging its inhabitants down with it.

> **Key quotation**
>
> DER ERSTE Leben?
> DER ZWEITE Vegetieren.
> DER DRITTE Krepieren.
> DER VIERTE Das ganze Städtchen.
> (*Act 1*)

The only hope that they can see is in a female billionaire, who is due to arrive at the town: 'DER ZWEITE Höchste Zeit, daß die Milliardärin kommt' (*Act 1*).

The regional train from Kaffigen stops at the station and the debt collector Glutz arrives, ready to repossess the town hall. The Mayor, the Teacher, the Priest and Alfred Ill approach the station from the direction of the town. The billionairess is due to arrive on the next scheduled train that stops at Güllen at 1.13 p.m. The visit by the debt collector comes somewhat unexpectedly and the Mayor is not impressed, but claims that there is nothing apart from an old typewriter that could be seized: 'Unsere Kassen sind leer. Kein Mensch bezahlt Steuern' (*Act 1*).

The debt collector is taken aback, as neighbouring towns are thriving. The Mayor agrees that it is something of an economic mystery but decides to let him carry on, as he would not want the debt collector to come after Claire Zachanassian's visit. The representatives of the town are convinced that the billionairess is their only hope.

They hope to persuade her, as a native of the town, to make a large donation to secure its future. Ill has been chosen to persuade her to donate money as he had a relationship with her when they were younger, when she was known as Klara Wäscher. The Priest alludes to a rumour about their split but Ill dismisses it with the words, 'Das Leben trennte uns, nur das Leben, wie es eben kommt' (Act 1).

The Mayor requests some details about Claire's youth for his dinner speech. The Teacher informs him that she had not performed well at school, apart from in botany and zoology. Ill remembers a few examples of her love for justice and her sense of charity. The Mayor informs Ill that the men of Güllen have agreed that Ill would become his successor, as he is the most popular person in the town.

- The town of Güllen is mysteriously impoverished.
- This part of Act 1 is key: it sets the context and alludes to many core aspects of the play that are later explored.
- Ill and the town dignitaries attempt to embellish Klara's past activities. At the same time, Ill does not reveal anything when asked by the Priest whether he has anything to confess. As the play unfolds, these lies will contribute to Ill's fate.
- It is made obvious that obtaining the donation is dependent on Ill. The audience assumes that Claire's love for justice will play a vital role as the plot develops.

> **Key quotation**
>
> ILL Klara liebte die Gerechtigkeit. Ausgesprochen. Einmal wurde ein Vagabund abgeführt. Sie bewarf den Polizisten mit Steinen.
>
> DER BÜRGERMEISTER Gerechtigkeitsliebe. Nicht schlecht. Wirkt immer. Aber die Geschichte mit dem Polizisten unterschlagen wir besser.
>
> ILL Wohltätig war sie auch. Was sie besaß, verteilte sie, stahl Kartoffeln für eine arme Witwe.
>
> DER BÜRGERMEISTER Sinn für Wohltätigkeit. Dies, meine Herren, muß ich unbedingt anbringen.
> (Act 1)

Aufgabe 1

Lesen Sie das Schlüsselzitat (,Key quotation') oben noch einmal. Welche Charaktereigenschaften werden Claire hier zugeschrieben? Warum lässt der Bürgermeister einige Details weg? Was will er damit bewirken?

Claire Zachanassian's arrival at Güllen: *'Glockenton*. DER ERSTE Der ›Rasende Roland‹ [...]'

The Gülleners think that they have approximately two hours left until Claire Zachanassian's arrival but to their surprise the express train comes to a halt at Güllen. The conductor questions Claire Zachanassian, who has pulled the emergency brake as she did not want to travel on the slower train. In order to calm down the conductor she offers him a thousand in cash. (As the play is set 'somewhere in Europe', Dürrenmatt avoids any references to a specific currency.) Claire also offers an additional sum of three thousand for the foundation for railway employees' widows. As this does not exist, she instructs the conductor to found one. This brief episode has given the Mayor and his fellow citizens the time to recover from the shock and as the train is departing, the Mayor welcomes Claire Zachanassian 'home': als ein Kind unserer Heimat ...' (*Act 1*).

Claire greets Ill and tells him that she has always intended to return to Güllen. Claire asks Ill to use the pet names that he used to call her ([...] Wildkätzchen [...] Zauberhexchen (*Act 1*)), while disagreeing that he is still her 'black panther'.

Key quotation

CLAIRE ZACHANASSIAN Ich nannte dich: mein schwarzer Panther.

ILL Der bin ich noch.

CLAIRE ZACHANASSIAN Unsinn. Du bist fett geworden. Und grau und versoffen.

ILL Doch du bist die gleiche geblieben. Zauberhexchen.
(*Act 1*)

Claire considers herself to be an old woman, her left leg having been replaced by a prosthesis following a car accident. Ill is introduced to her seventh husband Moby, an owner of tobacco plantations, whose first name is really Pedro; she has rechristened him, so that his name rhymes with that of her butler Boby. She points out the public lavatory built by her father and recalls how she sat upon its roof and spat at men.

Claire Zachanassian is greeted by the townspeople of Güllen, from the 1964 film adaptation, *The Visit*

After listening to a performance by the choir, Claire converses with the Police Officer and prophetically instructs him that he should not just turn a blind eye to some things, but possibly keep both eyes closed completely.

Key quotation

CLAIRE ZACHANASSIAN *mustert ihn [Polizisten]* [...] Aber vielleicht wird Güllen Sie nötig haben. Drücken Sie hin und wieder ein Auge zu?

DER POLIZIST Das schon, gnädige Frau. Wo käme ich in Güllen sonst hin?

CLAIRE ZACHANASSIAN Schließen Sie lieber beide.
(Act 1)

Due to the special guest's early arrival, the Mayor, ever conscious of his public façade, has to borrow the Teacher's top hat before introducing his grandchildren and his wife. When he introduces the Priest and the Doctor, Claire Zachanassian suggests to the surprised Priest that the death penalty might be reintroduced. She proposes to the Doctor that a future death certificate issued by him might give heart attack as the cause of death. Ill laughs at her jokes.

Before her bodyguards Roby and Toby take Claire to visit the two favourite places she and Ill shared in Güllen (the barn referred to as 'Petersche Scheune' and the local forest called 'Konradsweilerwald'), Claire instructs her entourage to carry her luggage to the hotel. This includes a coffin and a blank panther in a cage. Despite the citizens' unease, they all follow the coffin as in a funeral procession, accompanied by the ringing of the bells. As the Police Officer is about to follow, he meets two eccentric, blind characters within the old lady's entourage, namely the eunuchs Koby and Loby.

In front of the hotel, the Mayor, Priest and Teacher reflect on what has happened. While the Mayor is convinced that Ill will coax out millions from the billionairess, the Teacher anticipates some tragic events as he sees in her a goddess of fate.

- This part of Act 1 encompasses Claire's arrival with her unique entourage, as well as her first encounter with Ill.
- Her dramatic arrival (pulling the emergency brake and offering money to the conductor) is a sign of her power and of the power of money.
- Through her conversations with the Priest, the Police Officer and the Doctor, Claire prepares the citizens and the audience for tragic events in the future.
- The Teacher's analysis of Claire could be compared to a **foreshadowing** of evil. Throughout the play the Teacher will attempt to remind his fellow citizens of their moral beliefs.
- The witty, humorous and ambiguous dialogues are representative of the play's genre as a tragicomedy.

---

foreshadowing *die Vorahnung* a warning or suggestion of a future event

---

> **Key quotation**
>
> DER LEHRER Seit mehr denn zwei Jahrzehnten korrigiere ich die Latein- und Griechischübungen der Güllener Schüler, doch was Gruseln heißt, Bürgermeister, weiß ich erst seit einer Stunde. Schauerlich, wie sie aus dem Zuge stieg, die alte Dame mit ihren schwarzen Gewändern. Kommt mir vor wie eine **Parze**, wie eine griechische Schicksalsgöttin. Sollte **Klotho** heißen, nicht Claire, der traut man es noch zu, daß sie Lebensfäden spinnt. *(Act 1)*

Aufgabe 2

a. Lesen Sie das obige Zitat vom Lehrer noch einmal. Übersetzen Sie die folgenden Ausdrücke ins Englische:

   1. Sie kommt mir wie eine Parze vor.

   2. Claire könnte eine Schicksalsgöttin sein.

   3. Man sollte sie umbenennen.

   4. Der Lehrer traut ihr zu, dass sie Lebensfäden spinnt.

b. Was will der Lehrer mit der Aussage im Zitat oben andeuten? Notieren Sie sich Ihre Gedanken. Was könnte passieren?

Aufgabe 3

In diesem Abschnitt des ersten Akts werden mehrere Symbole verwendet, zum Beispiel der Panther und der Sarg.

a. Worauf weist der Sarg hin? Wofür steht der schwarze Panther?

b. Können Sie weitere Symbole finden?

Claire and Ill in the 'Konradsweilerwald': *'Sie stoßen an [...]'*

The Police Officer joins the Mayor, Teacher and Priest drinking schnapps. The Teacher compares Claire to **Lais** and thinks of Shakespeare's Romeo and Juliet, while the Mayor is wondering what they are doing in the forest but decides in the end that they should drink a toast to Ill, his successor and Güllen's saviour.

Some productions cast two actors for Claire: in the forest scenes she is played by her younger self

Parca *die Parze* female personification of destiny in ancient Roman religion and myth; the Romans identified the Parcae with the three Greek 'Fates'

Clotho *Klotho* one of the Greek goddesses of Fate; she was the spinner who spun the 'threads of life'

Lais *Lais von Korinth* a prostitute from Greek Mythology

Instead of a scene change, actors represent the plants and animals of the forest. Claire stops in front of a tree, played by one of the actors, on which a heart is engraved, featuring her and Ill's names. After dismissing her servants, the old lady recalls their past: where they kissed and made love when she was 17 and he nearly 20. While he married his current wife Mathilde Blumhard, she married the old man Zachanassian, who discovered her in a brothel in Hamburg. Ill argues that he only married Mathilde so that Claire could be free to seek her own fortune and that, if she had stayed, she would have been as ruined – financially – as he is. Their lives are full of contrasts: while Ill suggests that he lives in hell, Claire states that she herself has *become* hell. Ill has only been to Berlin and Ticino ('Tessin'), a region of Switzerland bordering Italy; Claire, meanwhile, has travelled the world, which she claims she owns: 'Weil sie mir gehört' (*Act 1*). Ill uses the opportunity to stress that Güllen requires millions, which Claire shrugs off as a small sum for her. Ill wishes that life hadn't separated them as he is still in love with her. He gets excited and touches Claire; in fact, her various prostheses. He mistakes a body-part fashioned out of ivory for the hand he kissed 45 years ago. She concludes their time in the forest by suggesting that she is invincible. Her eunuchs repeat this: 'Nicht umzubringen, nicht umzubringen' (*Act 1*).

- In this part of Act 1, the two protagonists are given the space to revisit their passion for each other 45 years ago. Allusions are made to the fact that Ill left Claire for another woman and Claire herself ended up in a brothel.

- Ill claims that he is still in love with her; Claire sees through the flattery, knowing that the town needs her millions.

- Dürrenmatt himself found the idea of two old people talking about love and sex on the stage rather awkward. By using actors to represent the forest scene, which is an alienation effect, any potential awkwardness is diffused by the incongruity of the situation.

Key quotation

ILL Wäre doch die Zeit aufgehoben, mein Zauberhexchen. Hätte uns doch das Leben nicht getrennt.

CLAIRE ZACHANASSIAN Das wünschest du?

ILL Dies, nur dies. Ich liebe dich doch! *Er küßt ihre rechte Hand*. Dieselbe kühle weiße Hand.

CLAIRE ZACHANASSIAN Irrtum. Auch eine Prothese. Elfenbein.
(*Act 1*)

Claire Zachanassian's husbands

At the time of her arrival in Güllen, Claire Zachanassian has been married seven times. The first husband, a billionaire, was the old man Zachanassian.

The first six of her husbands are not actually part of the play, though they are referred to briefly throughout: the second was the owner of 'Western Railway'; the third was a secretary of state for foreign affairs; the fourth was Lord Ismael; the fifth a fashion designer (the 'most beautiful' of all her husbands, who has designed all her wedding dresses); her sixth husband was a surgeon.

Her seventh husband Moby (actual name: Pedro) was the owner of tobacco plantations. Her eighth husband Hoby is a German film actor; Claire marries him in the church in Güllen. Her ninth husband is Zoby, a Nobel Laureate.

Aufgabe 4

a. Finden Sie das Gespräch unten zwischen Claire und Ill im ersten Akt, das im Konradsweilerwald stattfindet. Was erfahren wir über Ills Verhältnis zu seiner Frau? Was denkt er über seine Kinder?

Akt 1, Seite 38: *CLAIRE ZACHANASSIAN Du bist ruiniert? [...] ILL [...] Eine Reise nach Berlin und eine ins Tessin, das ist alles.*

b. Im Schlüsselzitat ('Key quotation') auf der vorherigen Seite gesteht Ill Claire, dass er sie noch immer liebe (S. 11). Was halten Sie von diesem Geständnis? Wie wird Ihrer Meinung nach seine Frau reagieren, wenn sie davon erfährt?

The official welcome and Claire Zachanassian's offer and conditions: *'Blasmusik ertönt, feierlich getragen [...]'*

The townspeople await Claire at the welcome dinner at the 'Goldener Apostel'. The town band and a male gymnast perform for the old lady, who is impressed by the latter's muscular body and asks whether he has strangled anyone previously. While Ill interprets these as witticisms, the Doctor is less sure and concludes, 'Solche Späße gehen durch Mark und Bein' (*Act 1*).

During the introduction of their wives to Claire, Ill whispers to the Mayor that Claire has promised millions. Claire also informs the Mayor that there is no need to wait for her husband, since he has gone fishing and she will divorce him anyway, as she wants her childhood dream to come true: to be married in the church of Güllen.

When all guests are seated, the Mayor opens the dinner with his speech. Despite all the negative occurrences in the world since her departure, he claims that the townspeople have never forgotten her and her parents. His speech is full of exaggeration, including the idea that her achievements in school are still held up as exemplary. He also narrates the story about her stealing potatoes for the old widow Boll somewhat favourably, to illustrate her sense of charity. He celebrates her charitable achievements and her social care projects across the world.

As the guests applaud, Claire thanks the Mayor for his kind words. She insists on correcting his euphemistic characterisation of her as a considerate teenager by recounting the real reason for stealing the potatoes: she wanted to sleep with Ill in the widow's bed and bribed her with the potatoes. She then proceeds to put forward her offer to Güllen.

> **Key quotation**
>
> CLAIRE ZACHANASSIAN [...] Um jedoch meinen Beitrag an eure Freude zu leisten, will ich gleich erklären, daß ich bereit bin, Güllen eine Milliarde zu schenken. Fünfhundert Millionen der Stadt und fünfhundert Millionen verteilt auf alle Familien.
> *(Act 1)*

Her offer of one billion is met with stunned silence, followed by exultation, but the latter is curtailed by her announcement of the condition that she wants justice in return. The announcement is met with more silence. The Mayor protests that justice cannot be bought, but Claire claims that everything can be bought and asks her butler Boby to speak. Boby reveals himself to be Mr Hofer, the former chief justice in Güllen. He explains that Claire Zachanassian, then Klara Wäscher, filed a paternity suit against Ill in 1910. Ill then denied being the father of Klara's child by bribing two witnesses to lie to the court: Jakob Hühnlein and Ludwig Sparr, who turn out to be known now as Koby and Loby, the two eunuchs. Both lied about having slept with Klara too. Later, Claire sought them out and had them blinded and castrated ('kastriert'). Claire then states that the child died a year later and that she became a prostitute because she lost the court case, and concludes that she can now afford to buy justice. She repeats her offer: '[...] Eine Milliarde für Güllen, wenn jemand Alfred Ill tötet' (*Act 1*).

Ill's wife rushes up to her husband with an emotional cry, while Ill himself tries to reason with Claire that life has since moved on, making retribution unnecessary. However, Claire does not accept this as she herself has forgotten nothing and wants justice for a billion. The Mayor rejects the offer in the name of humanity on behalf of the applauding townspeople, as they would rather stay poor than be responsible for the bloodshed of their fellow townsman. Claire is not discouraged and merely concludes Act 1 with the words, 'Ich warte' (*Act 1*).

- In the final part of Act 1, Claire reveals her offer and its condition: if someone kills her former lover Ill, she will donate one billion to Güllen and the citizens of Güllen.
- Ill's tainted past is exposed when Claire reveals how her paternity suit against him was dismissed because Ill betrayed her by bribing two men to lie in court.
- At this moment, the Mayor and townspeople appear repelled by Claire's offer.
- Claire's remark that she is waiting suggests she is anticipating a change of heart.

Key quotations

CLAIRE ZACHANASSIAN Ich will die Bedingung nennen. Ich gebe euch eine Milliarde und kaufe mir dafür die Gerechtigkeit.
(Act 1)

DER BÜRGERMEISTER Frau Zachanassian: Noch sind wir in Europa, noch sind wir keine Heiden. Ich lehne im Namen der Stadt Güllen das Angebot ab. Im Namen der Menschlichkeit. Lieber bleiben wir arm denn blutbefleckt.
(Act 1)

Aufgabe 5

Finden Sie die Textstelle unten und beantworten Sie die Fragen.

Akt 1, Seite 49: *ILL Zauberhexchen! [...] CLAIRE ZACHANASSIAN [...] Gerechtigkeit für eine Milliarde!*

a. Finden Sie im Text jene Ausdrücke, die Ihnen helfen, diese Redewendungen zu übersetzen:

1. you cannot demand
2. life went on
3. your betrayal
4. that we settle our score
5. to suspend time

b. Warum fordert Claire Zachanassian Ills Leben?

c. Was meint sie mit ‚Vergänglichkeit'? Erklären Sie das Wort auf Deutsch.

d. Ist dieses Angebot Ihrer Meinung nach vertretbar oder nicht? Warum (nicht)?

Aufgabe 6

a. Überlegen Sie sich, welche die wichtigsten Momente im ersten Akt sind. Dann fassen Sie den Inhalt des ersten Akts in nicht mehr als 150 Wörtern zusammen.

b. Im Laufe des ersten Akts gibt es mehrmals Hinweise darauf, dass Claire Zachanassian Ills Tod vorbereitet. Welche Zeichen und Textstellen weisen darauf hin? Erstellen Sie eine Liste oder eine Mindmap.

Tips for assessment

It is unlikely that you will be asked to summarise the events of the play as part of your final assessment. However, you will need to refer to the plot as part of your answer. Therefore, it is important for you to know what the key aspects of each act are.

Act 2

The first signs of a wealthier lifestyle and Claire's reflections on her husbands: *'Das Städtchen, nur angedeutet. [...]'*

Act 2 starts in Ill's shop, with Ill and his son observing Roby and Toby delivering wreaths which appear to be for a funeral. Son and father agree that no one need worry, because the town is supportive of Ill. However, neither Ill's wife nor his children have breakfast that morning with Ill, who sings his wife's praises and proclaims that his children are good.

The first customer Hofbauer selects some expensive cigarettes on credit. Ill allows him to do so, as he believes that, as citizens, they must stick together: '[...] weil wir zusammenhalten müssen' (Act 2). Two women buy full-cream milk, rather than the cheaper skimmed milk, and various other extravagant groceries on credit. While the women are eating their 'purchased' chocolate in Ill's shop, Ill and Hofbauer observe Claire Zachanassian and her butler on the hotel's balcony. Claire has now divorced her seventh husband and is engaged to a film actor. Just as Ill is observing that the town's rejection of her offer was the best hour of his life, 'der Zweite', another customer, arrives and reinforces that they are all fully in support of Ill.

> **Key quotation**
>
> DIE FRAUEN *Schokolade essend* Felsenfest, Herr Ill, felsenfest.
>
> DER ZWEITE Du bist schließlich die beliebteste Persönlichkeit.
>
> DER ERSTE Die wichtigste.
>
> DER ZWEITE Wirst im Frühling zum Bürgermeister gewählt.
>
> DER ERSTE Todsicher.
>
> DIE FRAUEN *Schokolade essend* Todsicher, Herr Ill, todsicher.
> (Act 2)

The customer demands cognac. Ill puts it on credit but expects payment next week when the unemployment benefits have been paid. Once Ill realises that 'der Zweite', as well as all the other people in his shop, are wearing new yellow shoes on credit, he loses his temper, throws goods at them and questions how they will pay: 'Womit wollt ihr zahlen? Womit wollt ihr zahlen? Womit? Womit?' (Act 2). While Hoby, Claire's eighth husband-to-be, comments on the noise coming from Ill's shop, reference is also made to the black panther, a present given to Claire by the Pasha of Marrakech, which is hissing loudly in another room.

- In the first scene of Act 2, the townpeople verbally express their full support for Ill, but their extravagant shopping actions contradict this support.

- While the members of Ill's family have already distanced themselves from Ill, he deludes himself into believing that his children are good and dutiful.
- Ill's outburst towards the end of the scene is mirrored by the black panther's hissing noises, demonstrating the symbolic link between them.

Key quotation

ILL Sie hat sich verrechnet. Ich bin ein alter Sünder, Hofbauer, wer ist dies nicht. Es war ein böser Jugendstreich, den ich ihr spielte, doch wie da alle den Antrag abgelehnt haben, die Güllener im ›Goldenen Apostel‹, einmütig, trotz dem Elend, war's die schönste Stunde in meinem Leben.
(Act 2)

Aufgabe 7

Was ist für Sie ein ‚Jugendstreich'? Nennen Sie Beispiele. Inwieweit stimmen Sie Ill zu, dass es sich bei der verleugneten Vaterschaftsklage um einen Jugendstreich handelte?

Aufgabe 8

Was will Dürrenmatt dem Publikum mit der Szene in Ills Laden vermitteln? Was bedeutet der Kaufrausch der Güllener?

Ill confronts the Police Officer and the hunt for the black panther begins: 'ILL Ihre Pflicht [...]'

Ill arrives at the police station and makes several attempts to demand Claire's arrest. The Police Officer claims that this request is itself rather peculiar. He refuses to instigate an arrest on the grounds that Claire's incitement to murder Ill cannot be taken seriously, considering the rather exaggerated reward offer of a billion. Ill stresses that he feels threatened by her proposal but once again the Police Officer claims not to comprehend Ill's worries: no one is actually attempting to murder him. Ill tries to explain to him that all the people's credit purchases constitute a sign, as they will not be able to pay without Claire's money.

When Ill asks the Police Officer directly how he intends to pay for his more expensive beer and new yellow shoes, he just replies that this is his own business ('Meine Angelegenheit' (Act 2)) and answers the phone. When the Police Officer picks up his rifle, Ill tells him that the town will pay for its debts through him. The Police Officer tells Ill he is making up stories and rushes off to hunt the black panther which has escaped. The Police Officer refers to the big cat as Claire's lapdog. Ill, however, is convinced that they are hunting him down.

While this scene at the police station takes place, Claire and her husband-to-be are on the balcony, opening letters from previous husbands and important world leaders including 'Ike' (US President Dwight Eisenhower) and Nehru (the first Prime Minister of India), congratulating them on their engagement. Butler Boby is instructed to get shares in Dupont, an American chemical company, bought up.

- The conversation with the Police Officer demonstrates to the audience that Ill is frightened and feels threatened.

- Dürrenmatt uses this dialogue to show that although Ill has grasped the situation fully, the Police Officer, who represents law and order, chooses to ignore any signs of potential danger for Ill, isolating him even from the protection of the law.

- Ill's final words in the scene are not just the start of the hunt for the panther and himself; they allude to future events.

Key quotations

ILL Die Stadt macht Schulden. Mit den Schulden steigt der Wohlstand. Mit dem Wohlstand die Notwendigkeit, mich zu töten. [...]
(Act 2)

DER POLIZIST Ich habe keine Zeit, über Ihre Hirngespinste zu disputieren, Mann. Ich muß gehen. Der verschrobenen Milliardärin ist das Schoßhündchen fortgelaufen. Der schwarze Panther. Ich muß ihn jagen. Das ganze Städtchen muß ihn jagen. *Er geht nach hinten hinaus.*

ILL Mich jagt ihr, mich.
(Act 2)

Aufgabe 9

Sie sind der Polizist. Auf der Jagd nach dem schwarzen Panther treffen Sie auf den Bürgermeister. Was erzählen Sie ihm? Verfassen Sie einen kurzen Dialog zwischen Ihnen und dem Bürgermeister.

Aufgabe 10

Denken Sie über diese Szene noch einmal genau nach. Diese Fragen dienen als Impuls:

- Was erfahren wir in dieser Szene?
- Was wird durch Ills Aussagen deutlich?
- Inwiefern ist Ills Angst berechtigt?
- Wie verhält sich der Polizist Ill gegenüber?
- Wo ist Ills Familie?
- Worauf will uns Dürrenmatt mit dieser Szene vorbereiten?

Aufgabe 11

Finden Sie die Textstelle unten im Theaterstück *Der Besuch der alten Dame*.

Akt 2, Seite 63: *ILL Der Vorschlag b e d r o h t mich [...]' DER POLIZIST [...] Ich muß ihnen nachträglich gratulieren.*

a. Übersetzen Sie dieses Zitat ins Englische.

b. Vergleichen Sie das Zitat mit dem Ende dieser Szene. Welche Rolle spielt das Gewehr, welche die Jagd?

c. Dieses Zitat enthält eine Vorahnung. Wenn Sie die nächste Szene des zweiten Akts lesen, denken Sie an dieses Zitat und überlegen Sie sich: Auf welche Handlung(en) wollte Dürrenmatt mit diesem Zitat im Voraus hinweisen?

Ill's conversations with the Mayor and the Priest: 'Rechts Verwandlung. Die Inschrift ›Stadthaus‹ [...]'

Ill calls on the Mayor next, who pretends to be busy organising the hunt for the black panther. The Mayor invites him to speak openly about his concerns but the initial conversation focuses on all the expensive purchases the Mayor has made. Ill admits that he is frightened. The Mayor is openly disappointed about Ill's distrust in his fellow citizens and the state. When Ill demands Claire's arrest, the Mayor responds with exactly the same words as the Police Officer: 'Merkwürdig. Äußerst merkwürdig' (*Act 2*). The Mayor then informs Ill that the town has decided that he is no longer a worthy candidate for the mayoral role and also that, while they do not agree with her, the citizens equally do not condone Ill's crime against Klara Wäscher. However, he tries to reassure Ill that their friendship will not be affected by this.

As Roby and Toby deliver more wreaths to decorate the coffin at the hotel, Ill is asked to remain silent but he argues that speaking up is his only chance to survive. The fact that Ill sees a potential threat in every single citizen of Güllen is met with outrage by the Mayor, who deems Ill to be libellous: 'Gegen diese Verleumdung protestiere ich im Namen der Stadt feierlich' (*Act 2*). When Ill discovers the architect's drawings of a new town hall, he claims that the Mayor has already sentenced him to death.

Claire's husband-to-be observes to her that he is getting depressed due to the smallness of Güllen. Ill enters the church to speak to the Priest. When Ill admits that he is frightened of the townspeople, the Priest argues that he need only be frightened of God. He insists that the hell to which Ill refers is within Ill, and that he should not be concerned about the purchases made by his fellow citizens, but rather about the immortality of his soul. When the sound of a new church bell becomes audible, Ill cannot believe that the Priest has also fallen victim to the spending spree. The Priest clings to Ill, then begs him to flee. He suggests that human beings are weak and that, should Ill remain in the town, someone will be tempted to kill him. When two shots are fired outside the church, Ill gets up, takes the Priest's rifle and leaves the stage.

- The conversations between Ill and the Mayor, and then the Priest, show that Ill's attempts to gain protection fail. While the Priest admits the weakness of human beings, the Mayor condemns Ill's past and plans a prosperous future for his town, without Ill.

- The audience is left wondering whether or not Ill will keep quiet or speak up in the remaining scenes.

- The dialogue with the Priest suggests that there is not much hope for Ill; his death seems certain. The question is, will he die as a hero or a villain?

Aufgabe 12

Welche Waren und Objekte werden im Laufe der beiden Gespräche genannt, die auf den zunehmenden Konsumrausch der Güllener hinweisen? Erstellen Sie eine Liste.

Aufgabe 13

Beantworten Sie die Fragen zu dieser Szene.

a. Warum spricht der Bürgermeister von ‚Undank' (*Akt 2, Seite 69*)?

b. Warum haben sich die Güllener dafür entschieden, Ill doch nicht zum Bürgermeister zu machen?

c. Warum soll Ill schweigen? Wie reagiert Ill auf diese Aufforderung? Warum?

d. Was meint der Pfarrer, wenn er sagt, dass die Hölle in Ill selbst liege (*Akt 2, Seite 74*)?

e. Warum rät er Ill zur Flucht?

ILL Ich fürchte mich.

DER PFARRER Fürchten? Wen?

ILL Die Menschen.

DER PFARRER Daß die Menschen Sie töten, Ill?

ILL Sie jagen mich wie ein wildes Tier.

DER PFARRER Man soll nicht die Menschen fürchten, sondern Gott, nicht den Tod des Leibes, den der Seele. [...]

ILL Es geht um mein Leben.

DER PFARRER Um Ihr ewiges Leben.
(Act 2)

DER PFARRER [...] Flieh! Wir sind schwach, Christen und Heiden. Flieh, die Glocke dröhnt in Güllen, die Glocke des Verrats. Flieh, führe uns nicht in Versuchung, indem du bleibst.
(Act 2)

Death of black panther and Ill's attempt to flee from Güllen: 'CLAIRE ZACHANASSIAN Boby, man schießt. [...]'

The panther is lying dead in front of Ill's shop. The townspeople offer condolences and perform funeral music for Claire beneath her balcony. Ill is outraged, as he sees it as a rehearsal for his own death. Ill bursts in on the citizens' chorus of tributes to the panther. As Claire thanks him for sparing her the ordeal of listening to the singing, and reflects on their romantic courtship, Ill grows increasingly agitated, pointing a rifle at her, then allowing it to drop again.

Claire is led back into her room by the butler to transfer a billion into her account. The stage scenery changes. The station is almost as it was at the start of the play, but with a new timetable and a holiday poster. Its backdrop however, is a burgeoning town, with cranes at work and new rooftops. Ill attempts to flee and catch the next train. His fellow citizens claim that they just want to accompany him to the station to wish him well. Ill explains that he intends to travel to Australia but the citizens claim that staying in Güllen would be safest for Ill. As the train arrives, well-wishers crowd around Ill. He feels suffocated and asks them to leave. Ill is convinced that one of them will hold him back when he attempts to board the train. The train departs and the citizens of Güllen leave the collapsed Ill behind on the platform. Ill knows that he is destined to die: 'Ich bin verloren' *(Act 2)*.

- The physical death of the black panther foreshadows Ill's own demise, since his pet name links the two symbolically.

- Ill's desperation is displayed when he threatens Claire with a rifle to try to force her to admit that it is all a horrible joke.
- Claire deflects Ill with talk of their earlier love, suggesting that she still loves him.
- Ill accepts his fate after the scene at the station, where his erstwhile friends intimidate him.

Key quotations

ILL Klara. Sag doch, daß du Komödie spielst, daß dies alles nicht wahr ist, was du verlangst. Sag es doch!

CLAIRE ZACHANASSIAN Wie seltsam, Alfred. Diese Erinnerungen. [...]

ILL Ich bin verzweifelt. Ich bin zu allem fähig. Ich warne dich, Klara. Ich bin zu allem entschlossen, wenn du jetzt nicht sagst, daß alles nur ein Spaß ist, ein grausamer Spaß. *Er richtet das Gewehr auf sie.*
(Act 2)

DER BÜRGERMEISTER Das ganze Städtchen begleitet Sie.

DER DRITTE Das ganze Städtchen!

DER VIERTE Das ganze Städtchen!

ILL Ich habe euch nicht hergebeten.

DER ZWEITE Wir werden doch noch von dir Abschied nehmen dürfen.

DER BÜRGERMEISTER Als alte Freunde.

ALLE Als alte Freunde! Als alte Freunde!
(Act 2)

Aufgabe 14

Lesen Sie die beiden Schlüsselzitate (oben) noch einmal.

a. Was will Dürrenmatt Ihrer Meinung nach dem Publikum mit diesen Dialogen mitteilen? Wie verhält sich Claire gegenüber Ill?

b. Welche Zweideutigkeit steckt in der Aussage ‚Wir werden doch noch von dir Abschied nehmen dürfen'?

Aufgabe 15

Verfassen Sie eine Zusammenfassung der Geschehnisse des zweiten Akts von 150 Wörtern. Bevor Sie diesen Text schreiben, überlegen Sie sich, welche Ereignisse für den Verlauf der Handlung am wichtigsten sind.

Act 3

Claire Zachanassian reveals the truth behind the poverty of Güllen to the Teacher and the Doctor: *'Petersche Scheune. Links sitzt […]'*

Following the high-society wedding of Claire and her eighth husband in the church of Güllen, Claire has retired to the Petersche barn to recuperate. The Teacher and the Doctor find her here. Claire informs them that she has already filed for her divorce from her newly-wedded husband and the two men explain to her that their fellow citizens have plunged themselves into debt. Claire stubbornly insists that they know what they must do: *'Ihr wißt, was zu tun ist'* (Act 3). The Teacher urges her to buy up all the run-down firms and industries, only to learn that Claire already owns them and instructed her agents to close them down some time ago in a plan to ruin the town. While the Doctor is shocked, the Teacher compares her to **Medea** and pleads for her to drop her pursuit of revenge and to show humanity. Claire argues that the world caused her to suffer as a prostitute and now, in revenge, she is turning the world into a brothel. The Doctor questions what they should do, to which the Teacher replies that they have to follow their conscience.

- The Teacher and Doctor discover that Claire owns everything in the city and orchestrated their poverty in revenge for what happened to her in the past.

- This scene makes clear that everything, even justice, can be bought.

- The townspeople are held up for criticism by Claire for holding their principles and values superficially, rather than really living by them.

Key quotations

CLAIRE ZACHANASSIAN […] Eure Hoffnung war ein Wahn, euer Ausharren sinnlos, eure Aufopferung Dummheit, euer ganzes Leben nutzlos vertan. *(Act 3)*

CLAIRE ZACHANASSIAN Die Menschlichkeit, meine Herren, ist für die Börse der Millionäre geschaffen, mit meiner Finanzkraft leistet man sich eine Weltordnung. Die Welt machte mich zu einer Hure, nun mache ich sie zu einem Bordell. Wer nicht blechen kann, muß hinhalten, will er mittanzen. Ihr wollt mittanzen. Anständig ist nur, wer zahlt, und ich zahle. Güllen für einen Mord, Konjunktur für eine Leiche. *(Act 3)*

Medea *Medea* a character from Greek mythology; in the play *Medea* by Euripides, Medea's husband Jason leaves her for another woman; she consequently kills the children she had had with Jason

Aufgabe 16

Lesen Sie diese Szene noch einmal. Welche Aussagen sind richtig (R), falsch (F) oder nicht im Text (N)?

a. Die Szene spielt im Hotel ‚Zum Goldenen Apostel'.

b. Gatte VIII ist bereits mit seinem Porsche abgereist und wird in der Ferne die Scheidung von Claire Zachanassian einreichen.

c. Claire besitzt die Wagnerwerke bereits seit mehr als vierzig Jahren.

d. Der Lehrer hätte eine neue Stelle außerhalb Güllens bekommen, hat sie aber nicht angenommen, weil er die Hoffnung auf eine Verbesserung der Lebensumstände in Güllen nicht aufgeben wollte.

e. Claire ist überzeugt, dass Milliardäre/Milliardärinnen so viel Geld haben, dass sie sich nicht um Menschlichkeit kümmern brauchen.

In Ill's newly decorated shop, the Gülleners air their concerns about Ill, speaking up to the press: *'Im Vordergrund rechts wird Ills Laden sichtbar […]'*

At Ill's newly-decorated shop, his wife and the customers talk about the pomp of Claire's recent wedding and the media presence in Güllen, while purchasing expensive goods on credit, including an axe. The citizens are concerned that Ill might speak up and reveal the situation to journalists. Ill's wife insists that her husband will not say anything, but seems unsettled by the thought that the town's fate could be jeopardised by careless words: 'Ich habe es schwer, Herr Hofbauer' (*Act 3*). The Teacher enters the shop and begins drinking. Journalists arrive and ask questions about Claire and her relationship with Ill. Ill's wife admits that her husband and the billionairess had been due to get married years ago, but lies about Ill's whereabouts. As the questioning continues, Ill's wife stresses that money alone does not lead to happiness: 'Geld allein macht nicht glücklich' (*Act 3*). Both of Ill's children, Karl and Ottilie, are present when the Teacher criticises Frau Ill, as well as her daughter, for betraying Ill; he foresees horrible consequences.

- The greed of the citizens is displayed when they pressurise Ill's wife into believing that Ill should not be allowed to reveal Claire's offer to the journalists.
- The moral struggle of some characters is revealed, such as the Teacher, who has turned to drink and accuses Ill's wife and daughter of betraying Ill.

Key quotations

DER ERSTE Wenn er Klara bloßstellen will, Lügen erzählen, sie hätte was auf seinen Tod geboten oder so, was doch nur ein Ausdruck des namenlosen Leids gewesen ist, müssen wir einschreiten.
(Act 3)

DER LEHRER Ich protestiere! Angesichts der Weltöffentlichkeit! Ungeheurerliche Dinge bereiten sich vor in Güllen!
(Act 3)

Ill's acceptance of his guilt and the Mayor's attempt to convince ill to commit suicide: *'Die Güllener stürzen sich auf ihn […]'*

While the assembled townspeople pounce on the Teacher, Ill appears at the top of the staircase and asks the Teacher to be silent, even though the Teacher is defending him. The journalists take a few pictures, including one of Ill with his family and one of him pretending to sell the axe. The journalists are distracted by the news that Claire has been seen with a new partner. The customers apologise to the Teacher but refer to Ill as a rascal or villain. The Teacher urges Ill to fight for his life and to speak up, but Ill is no longer prepared to fight: 'Ich kämpfe nicht mehr' *(Act 3)*. He accepts that he is guilty and therefore can help neither himself nor the townspeople. The tone of the Teacher's voice changes and he foretells Ill's murder. However, the Teacher also believes that the townspeople will have to face up to Ill's murder in the future, just as Ill has had to face up to his past. He buys another bottle of spirits and leaves the shop, while the members of Ill's family reappear. Ill admires the new shop and the Mayor enters. The two men discuss the looming municipal assembly later that evening and Ill agrees that he will accept the results of the vote on his death. The Mayor leaves a rifle for Ill, in the hope that he will commit suicide prior to the town meeting ('Gemeindeversammlung'). Ill, however, has overcome his fear and will accept their verdict. They will have to carry out their actions themselves.

- The Teacher attempts to speak up for Ill but Ill has accepted his fate.
- However, while Ill accepts his guilt, he is not prepared to commit suicide to make life easier for his fellow citizens.
- Ill's acceptance of the situation is reflected in his positive reaction to the changes made to his shop. He suggests a car trip with his family, their last ever outing together.

The townspeople take up arms

> **Key quotations**
>
> ILL Ich habe Klara zu dem gemacht, was sie ist, und mich zu dem, was ich bin, ein verschmierter windiger Krämer. Was soll ich tun, Lehrer von Güllen? Den Unschuldigen spielen?
> *(Act 3)*
>
> ILL Bürgermeister! Ich bin durch eine Hölle gegangen. [...] Aber nun schloß ich mich ein, besiegte meine Furcht. Allein. Es war schwer, nun ist es getan. Ein Zurück gibt es nicht. Ihr m ü ß t nun meine Richter sein. [...] Für mich ist es die Gerechtigkeit, was es für euch ist, weiß ich nicht. Gott gebe, daß ihr vor eurem Urteil besteht. Ihr könnt mich töten, [...] aber euer Handeln kann ich euch nicht abnehmen.
> *(Act 3)*

Aufgabe 17

Ills Kampf ist zu Ende. Warum gibt Ill den Kampf um sein Leben auf? Wie rechtfertigt er diese Entscheidung in dieser Szenenabfolge gegenüber dem Lehrer und dem Bürgermeister?

Aufgabe 18

a. Lesen Sie die Textstelle unten noch einmal. Wie beurteilen Sie diese Aussage von Frau Ill? Verfassen Sie eine kurze schriftliche Stellungnahme.

Akt 3, Seite 104–105: *FRAU ILL Alle machen Schulden, Fredi. [...] da hat es ein zu gutes Herz.*

b. Vergleichen Sie das Zitat in **Aufgabe a** mit der folgenden Aussage vom Lehrer. Verstehen Frau Ill und der Lehrer die Situation, in der sich Ill und die Güllener befinden, richtig?

Akt 3, Seite 103: *Bin nüchtern. Auf einmal. [...] Noch eine Flasche Steinhäger.*

Ill's last car trip with his family and the final encounter with Claire in the 'Konradsweilerwald': *'Die Frau kommt im Pelzmantel* [...]'

After the Mayor's departure, Ill's family members return, dressed up for their final trip together. Ill wants to see the town he spent all his life in for a final time and recognises all the improvements that have already been implemented since Claire's offer.

As they approach the forest, Ill decides to walk to the meeting through the forest and says his final goodbyes to his family, before they go off to the cinema.

Sitting on a bench in the forest, Ill is joined by Claire, who reveals that she is the owner of the 'Konradsweilerwald'. After Claire has sent her ninth husband Zoby away, she and Ill smoke and listen to Ill's favourite song. They talk about their daughter Geneviève, who was taken away from Claire at birth and who subsequently died. They reminisce too about how they saw each other when they were a young couple. Against the background of Roby's guitar melodies, Ill tells Claire that someone is bound to kill him at the assembly, even though he cannot say who it will be. Claire admits that she loved him but wants him ruined in order to resurrect her dream of being reunited with him in his death: she will keep him in a mausoleum (tomb) in Capri in her garden: '[...] Dort wirst du bleiben. Bei mir' (Act 3).

- Ill makes his final farewells to his beloved ones: his family and his love from the past. He does this against the backdrop of the woodland, which represents the idyllic nature of the past.

- He is comforted that his family members will not be taking part in his killing, as they are at the cinema, and this consolation helps him to face his murderers.

- For the first time, Claire unambiguously talks about Ill's demise being necessary to fulfil her dream.

Key quotation

ILL Heute abend versammelt sich die Gemeinde. Man wird mich zum Tode verurteilen, und einer wird mich töten. [...]

CLAIRE ZACHANASSIAN Ich liebte dich. Du hast mich verraten. Doch den Traum von Leben, von Liebe, von Vertrauen, diesen einst wirklichen Traum habe ich nicht vergessen. Ich will ihn wieder errichten mit meinen Milliarden, die Vergangenheit ändern, indem ich dich vernichte.
(Act 3)

Aufgabe 19

a. Übersetzen Sie das obige Zitat ins Englische. Welchen Traum will Claire Zachanassian verwirklichen? Wie will sie das machen?

b. Beantworten Sie die folgenden Fragen zu dieser Szene.

- Was erfahren wir über Ills Familie?

- Wie beschreiben Claire und Ill ihre eigene Jugend und sich selbst als Jugendliche?

- Welche Bedeutung hat Ihrer Meinung nach das Mausoleum?

The town meeting and Ill's death: *'Die Sänfte wird nach hinten getragen* [...]'

At the hotel's theatre hall, the men of Güllen take their seats on the stage, while their wives sit in the audience. A radio reporter explains the significance of the meeting that will be led by the Mayor in Claire's absence.

The Mayor opens his speech with Claire's gift of a billion, which is interpreted by the radio reporter as a social experiment: 'eines der größten sozialen Experimente unserer Epoche' (*Act 3*). The Teacher reminds the townspeople that the gift is linked to the condition of gaining justice. As they accepted one crime in the past, they will have to start living by their principles and values and put them into practice. He concludes his speech by reminding them that they are only allowed to accept this gift provided that they accept the billionairess's condition.

Following this speech, the Mayor praises Ill as he is the reason why this generous offer has been made, and Ill himself accepts this. No one asks Ill any questions, therefore the Mayor continues with the vote by asking the citizens to raise their hands: 'Wer reinen Herzens die Gerechtigkeit verwirklichen will, erhebe die Hand' (*Act 3*). Ill stays seated and all of the other citizens raise their hand and accept the gift, under the guise of leading a just life and saving their souls. The citizens chant a series of justifications for their imminent vote, causing Ill to deliver the emotional cry, 'Mein Gott' (*Act 3*). A technical problem with the press lighting necessitates the vote being repeated. Ill does not cry out a second time, as he is now aware of the citizens' attitude to him. The vote to accept Claire's gift is carried.

When the audience and press have left, the Mayor allows Ill a last wish to smoke a cigarette. The Priest tries to read Ill his last rites but Ill asks him to pray for Güllen instead. The men of Güllen form a human pathway for Ill to walk through. As he reaches the middle, they huddle around him. He ends up on the floor and the Doctor announces that Ill has died of a heart attack. The press interprets this as death from joy: 'Tod aus Freude' (*Act 3*). Immediately after this announcement, Claire hands over the cheque and departs for Capri with Ill, her 'schwarzer Panther', in the coffin.

The play concludes with a chorus from the newly-rich townspeople, lamenting poverty and its effects and celebrating the turning point in their fortunes through Claire Zachanassian and prosperity.

- The townspeople vote for justice, and consequently for Ill's death and murder.
- Ill, who in contrast to Claire has not been a hero from the start, becomes a hero during Act 3. He faces his fate bravely and has 'thrown off' his fear by accepting his guilt.

> **Key quotation**
>
> **DER BÜRGERMEISTER Die Stiftung der Claire Zachanassian ist angenommen. Einstimmig. Nicht des Geldes – [...] sondern der Gerechtigkeit wegen – [...] und aus Gewissensnot. [...] Denn wir können nicht leben, wenn wir ein Verbrechen unter uns dulden – [...] welches wir ausrotten müssen – [...] damit unsere Seelen nicht Schaden erleiden – [...] und unsere heiligsten Güter.**
> *(Act 3)*

 ## Aufgabe 20

Lesen Sie das folgende Zitat. Worauf spielt der Lehrer hier an? Erklären Sie, was der Lehrer mit diesem Zitat sagen will.

 Die Freiheit steht auf dem Spiel, wenn die Nächstenliebe verletzt, das Gebot, die Schwachen zu schützen, mißachtet, die Ehe beleidigt, ein Gericht getäuscht, eine junge Mutter ins Elend gestoßen wird.
(Act 3)

 ## Aufgabe 21

Stellen Sie sich vor, Sie sind Journalist und Claire Zachanassian gibt Ihnen ein Exklusivinterview. Welche Fragen würden Sie ihr stellen? Welche Fragen sind für Sie noch nicht beantwortet?

 ## Aufgabe 22

Die Güllener stimmen für die Milliarde, für Claires Angebot und damit auch für Ills Tod. Inwiefern stimmen sie für Gerechtigkeit? Was ist Ihre Meinung? Begründen Sie diese.

 ## Aufgabe 23

Fassen Sie die Geschehnisse des dritten Akts in einer Mindmap oder einem Diagramm Ihrer Wahl zusammen.

Structure

Der Besuch der alten Dame is written to be performed in three acts. Although the acts are informally subdivided into scenes, Dürrenmatt avoids using the title 'scene'. This is partly because the various scenes within the act are fluid and closely interconnected, but also because simple set changes are ongoing throughout.

Aufgabe 24

a. Erstellen Sie eine Tabelle, in der Sie die wichtigsten Ereignisse der drei Akte chronologisch darstellen.

	Wichtigste Handlungsabläufe	Was erfahren wir über die Vergangenheit von Claire und Ill?	Die für Sie wichtigsten Zitate
Akt 1			
Akt 2			
Akt 3			

b. Wie könnte man die jeweiligen Akte noch weiter unterteilen?

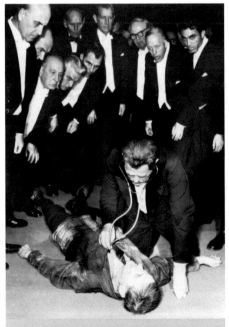

The doctor pronounces Ill dead due to a heart attack, as suggested by Claire

When analysing the structure of a play, **Freytag's Pyramid** of drama is often useful. The structure begins with the exposition stage ('die Exposition'), which sets the scene. An inciting moment ('das erregende Moment') heralds the next stage, the rising action ('steigende Handlung'), which builds to a climax ('Höhepunkt'). After the climax, the falling action ('fallende Handlung') follows, leading through to the final stage of resolution ('Lösung') or catastrophe ('Katastrophe').

> **Freytag's Pyramid** *Freytags Pyramide* the five-stage structure of a drama, illustrated by Gustav Freytag in 1863

Depending on the type of drama, extra stages might be added. The turning point ('Wendepunkt') is an important stage in *Der Besuch der alten Dame* as it is also closely linked with the development of the protagonist Alfred Ill. The diagram on the next page demonstrates how a version of Freytag's Pyramid can be used to describe the structure of this play.

Schauen Sie sich das Diagramm genau an und erklären Sie es auf Deutsch. Verwenden Sie zur Erklärung der Struktur dieser Tragikomödie die Begriffe der Freytags Pyramide.

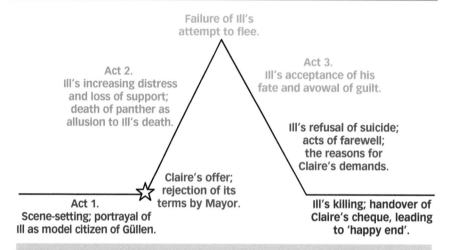

The various stages of *Der Besuch der alten Dame* using Freytag's Pyramid

Time

The play covers events over a period of more than 45 years. It is not clear how much time the townspeople take to act upon the old lady's request to kill their fellow citizen Ill. The visible changes to the buildings, for instance, let the audience assume that the time span the actual plot is covering is many months long. Claire's multiple marriages and divorces also support this.

Aufgabe 26

Erstellen Sie eine Zeittafel, die zeigt, wann welche Ereignisse stattgefunden haben. Vergessen Sie dabei nicht jene Ereignisse, die vor über vierzig Jahren passierten.

Setting and location

The play is set entirely in Güllen, a once-successful town which has become, by the beginning of the play, visibly run-down and ruined. Its name derives from the German word 'Gülle' and can be translated as 'liquid manure' or 'slurry'. Dürrenmatt intended this to convey both the visible debauchery that takes place there, but also its moral degeneration, as it is a place where murder is interpreted as justice. By the end of the play, Güllen will once again be transformed into a prosperous, shiny and economically well-off town, like its neighbouring towns. Dürrenmatt locates Güllen 'somewhere' in Europe.

It is the train station of Güllen in the opening and the closing scenes of the play that makes the transformation visible to the audience. While the train station can also be seen as a symbol for Güllen's connection to the world and Ill's only hope of escape from his murderers, it is also the location where Ill finally acknowledges he is lost, towards the end of Act 2.

The forest ('Konradsweilerwald') and a barn ('Petersche Scheune') are settings for the two protagonists' memories of their joint past and of their love story. Throughout the play, the forest is a background reserved only for Claire and Ill and their dialogues about the past, for the justification of Claire's terms and conditions, as well as their final farewell.

The hotel 'Zum Goldenen Apostel' is not only the temporary home of Claire, her husbands, her pet panther and her entourage, it is also the place where the hunt for her other 'black panther' (Ill) begins. It is there that she announces her 'gift' as well as its conditions, and where, finally, the townspeople accept Claire's offer and murder Ill. The nearby town hall, police station and church represent those places where any citizen of Güllen should find help if in distress. All three places end up being symbols of corrupt institutions and, consequently, places of unhelpfulness, ignorance and ungodliness. Even the church has a 'new bell' and is now corrupt.

One other place of significance in the play is Ill's shop. It is a sign of his past, as he married into a prosperous shopkeeper family, rather than struggling along with Klara Wäscher and an illegitimate child. At the same time, it is his home, where the audience soon witnesses that even his family abandon him. The shop could be seen as the place where transformation takes place: in the citizens' (consumerist) behaviour and also in their beliefs and values, which change while they are purchasing goods on credit. It is also the location where the Teacher wants to open the eyes of his fellow citizens, including Ill's family, but the transformed Ill stops him doing so. As a consequence, the Teacher joins his fellow citizens in fulfilling the old lady's request. Finally, it is within his own four walls that Ill stands up to the Mayor's demand for his suicide.

Aufgabe 27

Erstellen Sie eine Tabelle von allen oben genannten Orten. Lesen Sie noch einmal die Szenenbeschreibungen im Theaterstück. Wie werden die jeweiligen Orte beschrieben? Welche Bedeutung haben die Orte für die Struktur der Tragikomödie?

Ort/Akt/Szene	Beschreibungen	Bedeutung
Bahnhof (Akt I/Anfang)	Das Gebäude ist verwahrlost. An der Mauer hängt ein halb zerrissener Fahrplan. Daneben ein kleines Häuschen, eine öffentliche Toilettenanlage: kahl und fensterlos.	Ein Weg in die Stadt und aus der Stadt hinaus; allerdings nur für manche, denn nicht jeder Zug hält.
Hotel ‚Zum Goldenen Apostel' (Akt I/Ankunft im Hotel)	Die gesamte Einrichtung ist verschlissen, verstaubt, zerbrochen, etc.	Ein Zeichen des wirtschaftlichen Verfalls; die Unterkunft von Claire und ihrem Gefolge.

Aufgabe 28

Sehen Sie sich noch einmal die Spalte ‚Beschreibungen' aus der Tabelle oben an. Finden Sie passende Synonyme zu den Adjektiven und Verben in Ihrer Liste.

Writing about plot and structure

In your assessment tasks you will not be asked to write a summary of the plot ('Inhaltsangabe'). Instead, you will need to apply your knowledge of the plot ('Handlung') thoughtfully, so that you can make direct links between the essay task and the relevant elements of the plot of *Der Besuch der alten Dame*.

Your knowledge of the structure of the play can be relevant in many types of questions: for example, a discussion of Claire's character would be illuminated by considering her role in the inciting moment. The development of Ill as a character is structured by various stages of Freytag's Pyramid.

Useful phrases

Es gibt einen Zusammenhang zwischen … There is a connection between …

… ist ein wichtiger Teil der Handlung. … is an important part of the plot.

Im Laufe der Tragikomödie entfaltet sich … In the course of the tragicomedy … unfolds.

Die dreiteilige Struktur des Theaterstücks … The play's three-part structure …

Im Gegensatz zu dem, was im ersten Akt passiert, … In contrast to what happens in the first act …

Wie wir am Anfang/im ersten Akt/am Ende der Tragikomödie sehen, … As we see at the beginning/in the first act/at the end of the tragicomedy …

Der erste Akt spielt in … The events in the first act take place in …

Wir erfahren, dass … We learn that …

Der Schwerpunkt der Handlung liegt auf … The plot focuses on/The emphasis of the plot is on ….

Im Laufe der Geschichte … During the course of the story …

Am Ende des ersten Akts/Am Schluss des Theaterstücks empfindet der Zuschauer/das Publikum … At the end of the first act/At the end of the play the spectator/audience feels …

Vocabulary

die Anstiftung instigation, incitement

jemanden zu Meineid anstiften to incite someone to false oath

die Aufopferung sacrifice

aufschreiben lassen to buy on credit

ein Auge zudrücken to turn a blind eye

ausrotten to exterminate

die Bedingung condition

bestechen to bribe

die Bonmots (npl) witticisms

durch Mark und Bein gehen it goes right through me (figurative) / to pierce marrow and bone (literal)

eine Fahne haben to have alcoholic breath

fingierte Ladentüre simulated shop door

das Gefolge entourage

das Geheimnis secret

sich etwas gönnen to treat oneself to something

die (starke) Konjunktur (strong) economy

merkwürdig peculiar

das Naturgesetz law of nature

pfänden to impound

sanieren to refurbish, recapitalise

sich nach Hause scheren to clear off home

schwatzen to chat or to gossip

die Unsterblichkeit der Seele the immortality of the soul

verraten to betray

jemandes Verhaftung verlangen to demand someone's arrest

der Versuchung erliegen to give in to the temptation

zum Tode verurteilen to be sentenced to death

von Weltbedeutung sein to be of global significance

Biography of Friedrich Dürrenmatt

Friedrich Dürrenmatt

- Friedrich Dürrenmatt was born in Konolfingen, Switzerland in 1921. He was the second of three children. His father was a Protestant minister, his mother a Sunday school teacher.

- Dürrenmatt's early fascinations with astronomy and painting were inspired by family guests. He was an avid reader, although he performed poorly at school.

- In 1935 Dürrenmatt's family moved to Bern where he attended a Christian Preparatory school. Although he performed poorly at school, he was an avid reader. Despite his Christian upbringing, he felt disillusioned by God after the horror of the Second World War.

- In 1941 he studied art in Bern, then literature for two semesters, before embarking on a short career in the military.

- Returning to Bern in 1943, Dürrenmatt studied philosophy and decided to become a writer. He wrote his first play *Es steht geschrieben* in 1945. He met and married Lotti Geißler, an actor, in 1946. They had three children.

- Although neither *Es steht geschrieben* nor his second play *Der Blinde* were well received, Dürrenmatt began to be successful as a writer of radio plays ('Hörspiele'), detective stories and comedies such as *Romulus der Große*.

- In 1951 his family moved to Neuchâtel. From here, he wrote his novels *Der Richter und sein Henker* and *Der Verdacht*. *Der Besuch der alten Dame* was published in 1956. This play launched him to international acclaim: it was translated into 25 languages and enjoyed a successful run on Broadway. His other major success came in 1969 with *Die Physiker*.

- He became the second German-speaking playwright, after Bertolt Brecht, whose work was staged and discussed in the Soviet Union. (For more on Brecht, see pages 46–47.) He expressed views on political issues, such as Israel's cause during the Arab-Israeli conflicts of the 1960s, Switzerland's neutrality and the flaws of **capitalism** and **communism**.

- In 1969 he resigned as director of the Stadttheater in Basel after suffering a heart attack.

- He married the journalist Charlotte Kerr in 1984 after his first wife died in 1983. With her creative support, Dürrenmatt won several literary awards, including the Austrian National Prize for Literature.

- He suffered a second heart attack and died in December 1990.

Political and social context

Dürrenmatt was always keen for his tragicomedy *Der Besuch der alten Dame* to be seen as a 'timeless' piece of literature. However, given that it was published in 1956, as an audience we are automatically reminded of the post-WW2 period, its challenges and opportunities for the German speaking countries, Europe and the world. However, as the storyline spans well over 45 years, it is obvious that comparisons are also made with what life was like during and in between the two World Wars.

Dürrenmatt himself was 18 when the Second World War broke out. His work often reflects the horrors and tragedy of this time. *Der Besuch der alten Dame* reflects particularly on the question of followership of a charismatic leader, or of a leader who promises his/her people a better life. At the start of the drama, the audience can observe how the townspeople reflect on their dire situation. Their stagnation in a metaphorical town of slurry makes them vulnerable followers to the perceived better life offered by Claire.

Economic depression

After the First World War prices soared, particularly in Germany due to the war **reparations**; in the shops, a pound of sugar could be obtained for 2 million marks. German workers were paid with bags of paper money and it was not uncommon for a wage packet to contain 500 million marks. The Great Depression of the early 1930s left many ordinary Germans desperate.

A suggestion of this financial situation is made in the play when the citizens of Güllen are unable to afford luxuries. The surreal images of the German financial collapse are echoed in the wild spending that occurs in Act 2, when people realise that they can have goods that had been previously inaccessible. They do not pay with handfuls of worthless bank notes but with a signature to say that they will pay later, hoping Claire's money will materialise.

> **capitalism** *der Kapitalismus* an economic system and an ideology based on private ownership of the means of production and their operation for profit
>
> **communism** *der Kommunismus* a system of social organisation in which all property is owned by the community and each person contributes and receives according to his or her ability and needs
>
> **reparations** *die Entschädigungen/Reparationen* compensation for war damage paid by a defeated state

The economic miracle

Der Besuch der alten Dame premiered in 1956, 11 years after the end of the Second World War, when Germany was at peace with Europe, recovering from the war years. Large forces of unemployed workers, ex-servicemen and displaced persons were eager to rebuild their lives, working hard for low incomes. Many employers who were paying low wages ended up with surplus money that was then reinvested into the German economy. In addition, Germany benefited from the economic planning in its **occupied zones**. This led to a currency reform and the introduction of the *Deutsche Mark* in June 1948. By 1954, the **Federal Republic of Germany** (West Germany) had joined the Council of Europe, the West-European Union and **NATO**. Germans viewed the future with justifiable optimism.

West Germany's economy continued to flourish and the steady, upward trend was referred to as an economic miracle ('Wirtschaftswunder'). In *Der Besuch der alten Dame*, the references to economic improvements in neighbouring towns to Güllen leave the townspeople questioning why they are unable to partake in this growth. Their financial depression leaves them vulnerable to Claire's offer of unimaginable wealth.

The rise of consumerism

Dürrenmatt was born and raised in a rural district of Bern in Switzerland, called Konolfingen. He witnessed his native area develop from an agrarian and dairy landscape into urban zones during the late 1940s and 1950s.

The trains hardly stop at Güllen at the start of the play, symbolising the effect that the economic boom ('Hochkonjunktur') had upon rural communities. The play was written after Dürrenmatt had moved to Neuchâtel. In 1955 he was taking a train journey to visit his wife in hospital and started to think about two small village stations, Inn and Kerzers, which were on the express train route. Dürrenmatt considered how, should the train no longer stop at these stations, this would signify the beginning of the end for village life.

References to the countryside in the play, such as the 'Konradsweilerwald' and the 'Petersche Scheune' are intended to evoke nostalgic and romantic times in the lives of Ill and Klara. However, they have lost their appeal with the passage of time: *'Petersche Scheune* [...] *Ganz links eine Leiter, ferner Heuwagen, alte Droschke* [...] *Oben hangen Lumpen, vermoderte Säcke, riesige Spinnweben* [...]' (*Act 3*).

---

occcupied zones *die Besatzungszonen* at the end of the Second World War, Britain, the US, France and the Soviet Union divided Germany into four occupation zones between 1945 and 1952; the purpose was to assist Germany in its rebuilding but also to control Germany

German Mark *die Deutsche Mark* the 'Deutsche Mark' ('DM') replaced the 'Reichsmark' and remained West Germany's official currency until it was replaced by the Euro

Federal Republic of Germany *die Bundesrepublik Deutschland/BRD* in May 1949, as a result of mounting tensions between the Soviets and the Allied occupiers of Germany, the Federal Republic of Germany ('West Germany') was formally established as an independent nation

NATO *die NATO* the North Atlantic Treaty Organisation was created in 1949, to represent a military deterrent against the Soviet Union

collective *die Gemeinschaft/das Kollektiv* people acting as a group

The original subtitle to the play was: 'Comedy of the economic boom' ('Komödie der Hochkonjunktur'). While the townspeople in *Der Besuch der alten Dame* are clearly poor and bereft of material goods when the play begins, the arrival of Claire, with her promise of untold wealth to the townsfolk, heralds unexpected access to luxury products. By the 1950s, Swiss and German citizens were beginning to enjoy luxury goods such as Steinhäger gin, cigars, Opel Olympia cars, chocolate and television. Holidays were becoming accessible to all, both within Switzerland and Germany but also to warmer countries such as Italy. Claire's wish to take Ill's corpse to a specially-constructed mausoleum in Capri echoes this fascination with exotic locations. By Act 2 of the play, the station, once shabby and drab, has become adorned with travel posters.

Dürrenmatt's characters buy alcohol and tobacco on credit (in anticipation of imminent wealth), start to take tennis and language lessons and they acquire yellow shoes. The colour of the shoes may suggest gold and prosperity, yet also a rotten and corrupt **collective**. The identical shoes point to the dehumanising effects of consumerism and the loss of individuality. Members of the chorus frequently repeat each other's lines, to underline this collective vacuity.

Key quotation

ALLE Wo geht's denn hin?

ILL Zum Bahnhof.

DER BÜRGERMEISTER Wir begleiten Sie!

DER ERSTE Wir begleiten Sie!

DER ZWEITE Wir begleiten Sie!
(Act 2)

Dürrenmatt also roots his play about the power of money in an historical context by referring to letters sent to Claire by famous and powerful political figures such as 'Ike' Eisenhower and Prime Minister Nehru: 'CLAIRE ZACHANASSIAN [...] Ike schreibt. Nehru. Sie lassen gratulieren' *(Act 2)*.

The effect of Claire's generous cheque upon the lives of the people of Güllen is ironically summarised by Dürrenmatt in the final scene description of the play.

> **Key quotation**
>
> *Drückten die immer besseren Kleider den anwachsenden Wohlstand aus, diskret, unaufdringlich, doch immer weniger zu übersehen, wurde der Bühnenraum stets appetitlicher, veränderte er sich, stieg er in seiner sozialen Stufenleiter, als siedelte man von einem Armeleutequartier unmerklich in eine moderne wohlsituierte Stadt über [...] Die einst graue Welt hat sich in etwas technisch Blitzblankes, in Reichtum verwandelt, mündet in ein Welt-Happy-End ein.*
>
> *(Act 3)*

The happy ending of wealth and prosperity – the consumer paradise in Güllen – has been purchased through the sacrifice of a life.

> **Aufgabe 1**
>
> Wenn Sie Parallelen zwischen historischen Ereignissen und Ereignissen im Theaterstück ziehen wollen, können Sie Relativsätze benutzen. Setzen Sie die passenden Relativpronomen ein.
>
> **a.** Die Besatzungstruppen, _____ wirtschaftliche Unterstützung Deutschland wesentlich nützte, wurden nach dem Ende des Kalten Kriegs im März 1994 aufgelöst.
>
> **b.** Der Marshallplan, _____ vom amerikanischen Außenminister George C. Marshall am 5. Juni 1947 präsentiert wurde, sollte der Wirtschaft in Deutschland wieder auf die Beine helfen.
>
> **c.** Das millionste Exemplar des VW-Käfers, _____ ein Symbol für das Wirtschaftswunder wurde, rollte 1955 als vergoldetes Sondermodell im Werk Wolfsburg vom Band.
>
> **d.** Firmen wie Krupp, _____ durch Rüstungsproduktion im Zweiten Weltkrieg in Verruf gekommen waren, durch Bomben stark zerstört und nach Kriegsende demontiert wurden, erholten sich in den 50er-Jahren.
>
> **e.** Busunternehmer boten Fahrten auch für die an, _____ sich noch kein eigenes Auto leisten konnten.

Switzerland and capital punishment

When the townspeople learn that Ill must be killed if they are to accept Claire's generous offer, they are initially appalled. The murder of a citizen would constitute a criminal act.

Switzerland abolished capital punishment in 1937. Swiss military law continued to allow the death penalty for treason, even up to 1992; however, in reality no executions were carried out after the Second World War.

By the end of the play, which was written in 1956 when capital punishment was illegal in most of Europe, the townspeople agree to execute Ill on the grounds that his death will atone for his injustice to Klara. In taking his life, they secure their legacy.

Tips for assessment

When you are using contextual arguments in your essay, you may wish to present a counterargument too. Try using some of the following 'starter' phrases regularly in your writing to help you achieve a balanced discussion:

Auf der einen Seite … auf der anderen Seite … (*On the one hand … on the other hand …*)

Trotzdem … (*Nevertheless …*)

Dagegen … (*However/In contrast …*)

trotz (+ gen) (*in spite of* (+ noun))

Dies steht in starkem Kontrast zu (+ dat) … (*This is in stark contrast to …*)

Es gibt Vorteile/Nachteile … (*There are advantages/disadvantages …*)

Im Gegensatz dazu … (*By/In contrast, …*)

Women's rights

The presentation of Claire as a wronged woman can also prompt a feminist reading of the play. Her choices in her formative years raise questions about the role of women in society generally; not only how they were treated historically, but whether that treatment has advanced in modern society.

Consider, for example, that women did not achieve full suffrage or the right to vote in public in Switzerland until 1971 (in one district, not until 1990).

All the women of the town are conspicuous in their absence during the vote, having been sent to the gallery to await its outcome, following an old tradition.

> **Key quotation**
>
> DER RADIOSPRECHER […] Auf der Bühne, die sonst Vereinsanlässen dient und den Gastvorstellungen des Kalberstädter Schauspielhauses, versammeln sich die Männer. Nach alter Sitte – wie der Bürgermeister eben informierte. Die Frauen befinden sich im Zuschauerraum – auch dies Tradition.
> *(Act 3)*

Claire's missing right hand and left foot are symbols of her earlier lack of control of her destiny. She was forced by men during the sham paternity suit into leaving her village in disgrace, and then had to resort to prostitution.

> **Key quotation**
>
> CLAIRE ZACHANASSIAN Es war Winter, einst, als ich dieses Städtchen verließ, im Matrosenanzug, mit roten Zöpfen, hochschwanger, Einwohner grinsten mir nach. [...] Nun bin ich da. Nun stelle ich die Bedingung, diktiere das Geschäft.
> *(Act 3)*

The play shows, however, that she – a woman shamed by men and disfigured by the circumstances of her accidents – is nevertheless strong enough to achieve her own justice.

> **Aufgabe 2**
>
> Was ist Ihre Meinung zu den folgenden zwei Aussagen?
>
> a. ‚Dürrenmatt bewundert die alte Dame, die mit ihrem Scheck Gerechtigkeit kauft.‘
>
> b. ‚Einer alten Dame die Vollmacht zu geben, Gerechtigkeit zu kaufen, ist gefährlich.‘
>
> Verfassen Sie einen Text von ungefähr 150 Wörtern. Welche Aussage überzeugt Sie mehr? Begründen Sie Ihre Meinung mit Argumenten.

Religion

As the son of a church minister, who attended Christian schools and experienced parental pressure to follow his father's career path, Dürrenmatt ensures that religion – in the figure of the Priest – has a significant profile in the play. There is no state Church in Germany today, and since 1949 the national constitution has guaranteed freedom of faith and religion. Dürrenmatt's scepticism about 'pure' Christian values is demonstrated in the Priest's succumbing readily to the temptations of a new church bell in exchange for the life of a parishioner. A further indictment of the role of the Church might be seen in the reference to a Christian welfare group removing Klara's baby from her at birth.

The war years of human suffering, and the perpetration of so many crimes against humanity, caused Dürrenmatt to question Christianity. By the end of the play, the chorus pays homage to the delights of new wealth and makes the briefest reference to how the Church will figure in their new lives. They will attend church on Christmas Day.

Aufgabe 3

Dürrenmatt stellt immer wieder Verbindungen zur Bibel her. Inwiefern ist es Ihrer Meinung nach berechtigt, Ills Schicksal mit dem von Christus zu vergleichen? Beziehen Sie sich bei Ihrer Antwort auch auf Beispiele im Text, zum Beispiel:

- Plakat am Bahnhof (Passionsspiel in Oberammergau) (*Akt 2, Seite 80*)

- Musik bei Claires Hochzeit (Matthäuspassion) (*Akt 3, Seite 87*)

- Maler malt einen Christus (*Akt 3, Seite 95, Seite 99*).

Inwiefern vertritt der Pfarrer die Bibel?

The Cold War and the nuclear arms race

A part of Dürrenmatt's cynicism for the future of mankind lies in his perception that money mattered too much in the mid-20th century. However, another part of his pessimism stems from the sense of looming catastrophe in the world at that time, as tensions increased between the East and the West.

By the mid-1950s, Europe was caught up in the deteriorating relationships between the Soviet Union and the US. During the Second World War, the United States and the Soviet Union had fought together as allies. However, since the late 1940s, it had become apparent that the conquering Allies – France, Great Britain, the US and the Soviet Union – were organising their occupied territories of Germany in very different ways. The US was wary of Soviet communism and criticised the new **German Democratic Republic** and the tyrannical way in which the communist dictator, Joseph Stalin, ruled the Soviet Union until his death in 1953.

German Democratic Republic *die Deutsche Demokratische Republik/DDR*
'East Germany' was established in 1949 from the area of Germany that was occupied by the Soviet Union

The Soviets, for their part, objected to the US's refusal to treat the Soviet Union as a legitimate part of the international community and, as the Soviet Union had sustained catastrophic losses of life in the Second World War, the Soviets blamed much of this loss on the US's delayed entry into the war.

After the war, such grievances escalated into deep mutual distrust and enmity. The US thought that the Soviet Union planned to control the world and the Soviet Union watched the arms build-up in the US with growing tension.

The Cold War ('der Kalte Krieg') is the name given to the relationship which developed between the US and the Soviet Union. It came to dominate international affairs for decades and was the subject matter of many espionage novels and films.

The most worrying aspect of the tension was the development of nuclear weapons. When the US exploded the hydrogen bomb ('H-bombe') in 1952, the Soviets responded with the production of their own extremely powerful nuclear weapon in the following year. In *Der Besuch der alten Dame*, the citizens speak of 'Der sonnenhafte Pilz der Atombombe' (*Act 3*) in their final chorus, a bleak note to finish on.

Dürrenmatt became politically involved in criticising both the capitalism of the west and the communism of the east. His play reflects his belief that ordinary citizens are powerless to change society.

The play's relevance today

Der Besuch der alten Dame was the literary work which gained Dürrenmatt international recognition. It is still performed regularly today and continues to be studied as a socially relevant work. The play's relevance today ('die Relevanz des Stücks für die Gegenwart') stems from its critique of human behaviour, which links to topics such as social responsibility, poverty, law and justice and the ethics of the media and press.

Dürrenmatt used unsettling humour and the grotesque (*die Groteske*) (see page 43) to point out the contrasts and contradictions of society, its morality, mistakes and deficiencies.

All citizens must submit to the rule of law, which gives order and structure to a society by fostering justice, and is generally upheld by governing bodies. However, Claire arrives and imposes her own version of the rule of law. As she possesses supreme wealth, she feels that it is only a question of time before she can achieve justice. Dürrenmatt suggests that money buys anything and can be seen to corrupt even the most morally-strong people. The play is a mind-game ('Gedankenspiel'). It shows how people can be seduced by power and money. It shows how a crisis, such as extreme poverty, can make people susceptible to temptation and how moral principles may cease to function when pitted against the prospect of material gain.

Aufgabe 4

‚Mit Geld kann man alles kaufen.'

Inwiefern trifft diese Aussage auf dieses Theaterstück zu? Wenn Sie Notizen machen, versuchen Sie auch neue Vokabeln zu verwenden.

Genre

Tragicomedy

Friedrich Dürrenmatt described his play as a tragicomedy ('Tragikomödie'). Tragicomedy can be seen either as a tragic play which contains enough comic elements to lighten the overall mood, or else as a serious play with a happy ending. *Der Besuch der alten Dame* contains both tragic and comic elements ('tragikomische Elemente').

The comic moments of the play can be emphasisd in staging: here, Husband VIII is sandwiched between Claire and Ill

Dürrenmatt suggested that tragicomedy was an appropriate genre ('Gattung') for the 20th century. By the 1950s, Europe was on the brink of the Cold War, with the threat of nuclear attack never far from the news. On the other hand, Europe had started to recover from the Second World War and was becoming defined by new wealth and prosperity. Whereas human beings may have lived previously within communities bound together by religious faith and security, in the modern nuclear age, clear definitions of good and evil no longer existed; such securities had been removed and, in Dürrenmatt's opinion, their removal made the world senseless. Just before he completed *Der Besuch der alten Dame*, he wrote:

 The world (and thus the stage, which represents the world) is monstrous to me, a riddle of misfortunes that we must accept, but before which we must not surrender.

translated from the essay *Theaterprobleme* by Friedrich Dürrenmatt, 1955

Grotesque comedy

Der Besuch der alten Dame communicates Dürrenmatt's frustration with the world. Black, grotesque humour ('die Groteske') is used to depict the ridiculous, chaotic nature of modern society. It makes the audience smile but, at the same time, feel uncomfortable, experiencing a sense of unease, which Dürrenmatt had intended. The richest, most powerful woman in the world, whose buying power appears infinite, is portrayed as a semi-repellent figure, whose numerous accidents have led to her needing prosthetic limbs. When Ill playfuly slaps her left thigh, he has to withdraw his hand in pain because he has hit the hinge of her false leg by mistake.

ILL *begeistert* Wildkätzchen! *Er schlägt ihr gerührt auf ihren linken Schenkel und zieht die Hand schmerzerfüllt zurück.*

CLAIRE ZACHANASSIAN Das schmerzt. Du hast auf ein Scharnier meiner Prothese geschlagen.
(Act 1)

Dürrenmatt emphasises the comic side of Claire's physical decrepitude further, when she is reassembling her body and has to tell her butler where to find her left leg: 'Hinter den Verlobungsblumen auf der Kommode' *(Act 2)*. The fact that her leg is hidden behind flowers which celebrate her latest engagement reinforces the grotesqueness of the moment.

Further touches of absurdity can be seen in the comic appearance of Claire's entourage. The two blind, child-like eunuchs, the gum-chewing gangsters and the butler wearing sun glasses appear with the ominous coffin at regular intervals throughout the play; grim reminders of how Claire has wreaked revenge on those who trespassed against her. The farce ('die Farce') of the final judgement scene, which has to be replayed because the attendant press had failed to connect the lighting system, again reinforces the chaotic nature of the society which Dürrenmatt is criticising.

Tragic elements

The play poses the question as to whether tragedy is still possible in the 20th century. The Teacher refers to ancient greatness ('antike Größe'), to the fates and to Clotho, who weaves the threads of destiny. Death and revenge step out of the train in Act 1, in the form of Claire Zachanassian. She is a tragic figure herself inasmuch as she has sufferered in her youth at the hands of malicious and exploitative men. She is the embodiment of an avenging angel. Dürrenmatt compared her to the figure of Medea in Greek tragedy.

Claire Zachanassian stellt weder die Gerechtigkeit dar noch den Marshallplan oder gar die Apokalypse, sie sei nur das, was sie ist, die reichste Frau der Welt, durch ihr Vermögen in der Lage, wie eine Heldin der griechischen Tragödie zu handeln, absolut, grausam, wie Medea etwa.
(Anhang, Anmerkung 1)

The comparison with Medea seems very apt, as in the play by Euripides, Medea avenges herself for the unfaithfulness of her husband, Jason, by murdering their children. When Medea erupts into tears at the mention of her children, she could simply be acting her part to elicit more of Jason's sympathy, or she could also be struggling internally with the decision she has made to murder them. There are moments in Dürrenmatt's play when Claire appears to regret that Ill must die. She has, however, adhered absolutely to her desire for justice and revenge, pursuing the two men who lied about her in court and having them castrated and enslaved.

Ill develops into a tragic hero who has fallen from a popular, assured position in society due to a fatal error of judgement made in his youth. Ill reaches a moment of **anagnorisis** in Act 3, when he accepts his own guilt and his fate as inevitable, just like a hero in Greek tragedy.

> **Key quotation**
>
> ILL Heute abend versammelt sich die Gemeinde. Man wird mich zum Tode verurteilen, und einer wird mich töten. Ich weiß nicht, wer er sein wird und wo es geschehen wird, ich weiß nur, daß ich ein sinnloses Leben beende. *(Act 3)*

He accepts this with calm and moral superiority, refusing to take his own life. He achieves greatness in death, whereas the Gülleners experience a moral death by accepting Claire's offer.

Dürrenmatt makes Ill into a tragic figure who is killed by fate, not by the classical divine fate, but rather by a fate comprising human flaws, particularly greed. Dürrenmatt does not present any answer to the problems explored in the play, but seeks to provoke his audience into thinking about what it has just witnessed on the stage.

The Greek chorus

By the end of the play, Ill has transformed into a tragic hero

While Claire Zachanassian and Alfred Ill are the protagonists in the play, a third, and very important, component is the chorus of Güllen citizens. The chorus was a traditional part of classical Greek theatre, which embodied collective morality and represented the voice of the public. The chorus consisted of between 12 and 50 players, who danced, sang or spoke their lines in unison and sometimes wore masks. In Dürrenmatt's play, the citizens of Güllen function as a Greek chorus, informing the audience in the opening scene of the economic struggles of the village.

> **Key quotation**
>
> DER DRITTE Ruiniert.
>
> DER VIERTE Die Wagnerwerke zusammengekracht.
>
> DER ERSTE Bockmann bankrott.
>
> DER ZWEITE Die Platz-an-der Sonne-Hütte eingegangen.
> *(Act 1)*

anagnorisis *die Anagnorisis* the point, especially in Greek tragedy, when a character comes to a realisation about his or her true identity or situation, or that of another character

The chorus comments with a collective voice on the dramatic action: for example, when they pledge their allegiance to Ill.

> **Key quotation**
>
> DER ERSTE Wir stehen eben zu Ihnen. Zu unserem Ill. Felsenfest.
>
> DIE FRAUEN *Schokolade essend* Felsenfest, Herr Ill, felsenfest.
>
> DER ZWEITE Du bist schließlich die beliebteste Persönlichkeit.
> *(Act 2)*

However, the chorus also embodies the collective mindlessness of consumerism, the weakness of authority faced with material temptation, and the disorder just beneath the surface of social order. When the black panther is killed, the chorus, led by the schoolmaster, is prepared to sing a funereal ode to the animal. However, Ill recognises it as a rehearsal for his own funeral and forbids the performance. At the end of the play, the townspeople appear as much slaves as they did at the beginning, 'progressing' from victims of poverty to captives of prosperity. Their final chorus begins with the words: 'Ungeheuer ist viel' *(Act 3)*. The citizens of Güllen quote word for word the beginning of Act 2 in Sophocles' tragedy *Antigone*, written between 496 and 406 BC, which says 'many things are dreadful but nothing more dreadful than mankind'.

In contrast, Dürrenmatt's chorus sings of things that are dreadful, the most dreadful of all being poverty.

> **Key quotation**
>
> CHOR I Ungeheuer ist viel [....]
>
> CHOR II Doch nichts ist ungeheuerer als die Armut
> *(Act 3)*

> **Aufgabe 5**
>
> Finden Sie die Fernsehversion des Theaterstücks aus dem Jahr 1959 auf YouTube. Schauen Sie sich die letzten Minuten an, in denen Claire den Scheck überreicht. Wie wird der Chor dargestellt? Wie reagieren Sie auf die Freude der Güllener, dass sie endlich reich sind?

The influence of Bertolt Brecht

Dürrenmatt was very interested in the dramatic theories of **Bertolt Brecht**, who died in the year that *Der Besuch der alten Dame* was published. Like Brecht, he wanted to create a distance between the audience and the events on stage, so that the audience was able to think about the play's message.

In contrast to Brecht, Dürrenmatt did not want to present ideologies or philosophies. Brecht saw drama as a way of changing society and his plays deliver a message, frequently a **Marxist** one. Dürrenmatt uses Brecht's theatrical ideas but refuses to make his plays into moralising experiences.

In traditional realistic theatre, events and characters are presented in realistic ways and the audience engages and becomes emotionally attached to them. Brecht's theory of **epic theatre** reacts against this, to encourage the audience to think about the wider message of the play and to criticise (not simply watch) what unfolds before them. Actors were trained to act as their characters, yet also communicate that they were actors playing a role, in a concept he called 'alienation effect' ('Verfremdungseffekt'). Production techniques included: simplified, non-realistic sets; announcements or visual captions which summarised the action; and intentionally interrupting the action with choruses at key junctures.

> **Bertolt Brecht** an influential German poet, playwright and theatrical reformer whose epic theatre developed drama as a social and ideological forum for left-wing causes
>
> **Marxist** *marxistisch* following the political and economic philosophy of Karl Marx and Friedrich Engels, which forms the basis of communism; a central Marxist idea is that of class struggle, through which oppression of the working classes should be overcome to create a classless society
>
> **epic theatre** *das epische Theater* the style and techniques developed by Bertolt Brecht, used to allow an audience to maintain an emotional objectivity necessary to learn the truth about their society

In *Der Besuch der alten Dame,* Dürrenmatt uses epic theatre effects on many occasions:

- In Act 1, townspeople become trees in a forest, with one wearing a heart around his neck to depict the place where Klara and Ill carved their names in the bark.
- Claire's husbands are made to appear interchangeable and unremarkable by the stage instruction in Act 2 that states that one actor could play several of them.
- In Act 3, a car, symbol of the new wealth acquired by Ill's family on credit, is depicted by using four chairs on the stage.

Aufgabe 6

a. Übersetzen Sie die folgenden Beispiele des Verfremdungseffektes ins Englische:

1. Die humoreske und erniedrigende Namensgebung der Männer in Claires Gefolge (Toby, Roby usw.) ist beispielhaft für den Verfremdungseffekt.

2. Die Erinnerung an die Liebesszene der Jugend enthält einen potenziell erotischen Moment, aber das überm Bein hochgezogene Kleid zeigt eine ‚hübsche' Prothese.

3. Der vom Lehrer versammelte Chor mit seinem Volkslied zu Ehren der Zachanassian bleibt ungehört, weil in diesem Augenblick ein Zug durch den Bahnhof rast.

b. Ergänzen Sie die Lücken im folgenden Text, der die Stile von Brecht und Dürrenmatt vergleicht.

Obwohl der ¹_____ ein Begriff der Brechtschen ²_____ ist, benutzt Dürrenmatt auch das Mittel der Verfremdung. Seine ³_____ spielen in der ⁴_____ und schaffen Distanz durch groteske Elemente. Was Dürrenmatt von Brecht unterscheidet, ist der ⁵_____ an die Veränderbarkeit bzw. Unveränderbarkeit der Welt. Dürrenmatt selbst meint, dass Brecht an eine ⁶_____ glaube, die veränderbar sei. Dürrenmatt ist jedoch überzeugt, dass die Welt sich durch die ⁷_____ verändere, aber der Mensch verändere sich nicht und falle daher der durch ihn veränderten Welt zum ⁸_____.

a. Welt	**b.** Gegenwart	**c.** Menschen	**d.** Glaube
e. Opfer	**f.** Dramaturgie	**g.** Komödien	**h.** Verfremdungseffekt

Writing about context

A well-formulated exam question will give you the opportunity to show off your knowledge of the novel. It may also offer you the chance to showcase your background reading. Before the exam, try to summarise the contexts which you consider to be particularly relevant into a series of easily-remembered bullet points. So, if the question reads

> **Wie bedeutsam ist die Gestaltung des Konradsweilerwalds und des Balkons im ‚Goldenen Apostel' im Theaterstück?**

you will want to cross-reference examples in the play with your knowledge of this particular context. You could mention that the scenes that take place in the woodland and in the barn are places of nostalgia, which recall the love that Ill and Klara shared before he betrayed her. You could include a reference to how Dürrenmatt felt about his native Switzerland, how he regretted that rural communities were being destroyed by industrial progress. In any exam question you will gain marks by giving clear examples of context: critical analysis of social contexts should be demonstrated through convincing interpretations and regular points of view, justified with evidence from the play.

Useful phrases

Dagegen lässt sich einwenden, dass ... One objection to this is that ...

Ich komme unweigerlich zu dem Schluss, dass ... I inevitably come to the conclusion that ...

Der Dramatiker benutzt/verwendet ... The playwright uses ...

... um seine Intention klarzumachen ... in order to make his intention clear

Um seine Ideen zu übermitteln, verwendet Dürrenmatt Stilmittel wie ... In order to put across his ideas, Dürrenmatt uses stylistic means such as ...

Das Theaterstück spielt vor dem Hintergrund eines Wirtschaftsaufschwungs. The play is set against a background of economic recovery.

Während der Hochkonjunktur fingen die Menschen damit an, ... During the boom people began to ...

Indem die Güllener Ill töten, sichern sie sich ihre finanzielle Erbschaft. By killing Ill, the citizens of Güllen secure their financial legacy.

Das Theaterstück kann auch aus einem feministischen Blickwinkel betrachtet werden. The play can also be viewed from a feminist perpective.

Trotz ihrer körperlichen Entstellungen und trotz der Erniedrigungen in der Vergangenheit, ... Despite her physical disfigurements and despite the humiliations of her past, ...

Vocabulary

archetypisch archetypal

auswählen to select

sich befassen mit to deal with

die Biographie des Dramatikers/Autors the biography of the playwright/author

das Frauenstimmrecht female suffrage

gegenseitiges Misstrauen mutual distrust

der Hintergrund background

die Hochkonjunktur boom

der Kalte Krieg Cold War

auf Kredit/Pump kaufen to buy on credit

die Lebensgeschichte life story

nachforschen to investigate

eine Rolle spielen to play a role

die Rüstungsproduktion arms production

sichern to secure

die damaligen Umstände/die Umstände zu dieser Zeit (mpl) the circumstances at that time

eine Verbindung herstellen to establish a link

im Vergleich zu in comparison to

die Verkörperung eines Racheengels embodiment of an avenging angel

die wirtschaftliche Unterstützung economic support

das Wirtschaftswunder economic miracle

die Zerstörung der natürlichen Landschaft destruction of the countryside

der Zusammenhang context

Main characters

Alfred Ill

In contrast to the complex yet static character of Claire, Ill is a figure who develops and progresses during the play. Dürrenmatt chose his name as a play on words, 'ill' being recognisable to his educated English-speaking audiences as an English synonym for 'sickly' or 'unwell'.

When the play begins, Ill is a 65-year-old man, who runs and owns a small grocer's shop, which he secured through his marriage to a local girl, Mathilde Blumhard. They have two children, Karl and Ottilie, who are in their early 20s. Ill tries to have a good relationship with his children, although he confides to Claire that they are both without ideals: 'Ohne Sinn für Ideale' (Act 1).

Alfred Ill, played by Anthony Quinn, in the 1964 film adaptation, *The Visit*

Ill's backstory

Through a series of asides to the townspeople, and in his sentimental reflections with Claire, the audience learns about Ill's earlier life. When he was 20, he fell in love with a local girl, Klara Wäscher, and they enjoyed a passionate love affair which they conducted in the woods, in the barn and in the house of an elderly widow, whom they bribed with potatoes to allow them the use of her bed. Ill's friends used to follow the couple around, although Ill threw stones at them to try to discourage them. Ill was clearly a handsome 'catch' for Klara, as she referred to him then as her 'black panther'.

Once Klara realised that she was pregnant, Ill became reluctant to continue the relationship, so Klara was obliged to pursue a paternity suit. He bribed his friends to give false evidence and say that they too had had sexual relations with her. Ill thus freed himself of the responsibility for the baby and condemned Klara to a life of prostitution.

Ill then married Mathilde, whose family grocery shop he duly inherited. They had a family and he remained an 'upright' citizen of Güllen. Unlike Claire, who has since travelled the world, the audience is told that Ill has only twice left the town.

Ill as the carrier of the town's hopes

At the beginning of Act 1, Ill is considered a popular man in the town and he has been nominated to have a special role in the meeting and greeting of Claire Zachanassian from the train. It is made clear to the audience that his previous relationship with her, referred to vaguely by the Priest as 'eine unbestimmte Geschichte' (Act 1), will play a pivotal part in securing money from the billionairess.

> DER BÜRGERMEISTER [...] das übrige muß Ill tun.
> ILL Ich weiß. Die Zachanassian soll mit ihren Millionen herausrücken.
> *(Act 1)*

In an example of **dramatic irony**, the Mayor observes that everything depends on Ill's ability to take advantage of his previous relationship with Klara: 'Sie waren mit ihr befreundet, Ill, da hängt alles von Ihnen ab' (*Act 1*). In the end, everything depends on Ill, inasmuch as his death will precipitate untold wealth for the town.

Ill is proud and flattered by the importance of his role in the welcome committee, as carrier of the town's hope ('der Hoffnungsträger'). He is convinced that he is still a virile and attractive man, making sexual insinuations about having the money in the bag for the citizens, as a result of having slept with Klara: 'Sehen Sie, Herr Lehrer, d i e habe ich im Sack' (*Act 1*). His exaggerated self-esteem is also made very clear when he informs Claire that he is still the black panther to which she referred when they were lovers.

> **dramatic irony** *die dramatische Ironie* a technique by which the full significance of words and actions on stage becomes clear to the audience but not to the character(s)

In conversation with Claire in the woods, Ill reveals himself to be a sycophantic liar, claiming that he left her (when she was pregnant) in order not to get in her way. The audience may not, at this early stage in the play, be able to decide whether these excuses are those of a self-deluded man who actually believes that he made a big sacrifice in abandoning Klara, or whether he is fabricating lies at a rapid pace in order to secure Claire's investment. He already knows that his chances of becoming the next mayor rest upon his success. Swept along by the nostalgia of his and Claire's reminiscences in the wood, Ill does indeed appear to have loved her. However, the memories have become romantic clichés and he is prepared to dismiss any errors of judgement that he made at the time, as those of two people who were 'jung und hitzig' (*Act 1*).

> ILL Wäre doch die Zeit aufgehoben, mein Zauberhexchen. Hätte uns doch das Leben nicht getrennt.
> CLAIRE ZACHANASSIAN Das wünschest du?
> Ill Dies, nur dies. Ich liebe dich doch!
> *(Act 1)*

When he is confronted about his bribery of witnesses and manipulation of the truth by the former judge, Ill changes his strategy. He refuses to take responsibility for his past actions, claiming that the exploitation of Klara is a story that is over and done with. His reaction, however, has changed from a complacent one, as he implied that he had done Klara a favour in letting her leave the town, to an exasperated one, which seeks to ignore what happened: 'ILL *stampft auf den Boden* Verjährt, alles verjährt! Eine alte, verrückte Geschichte' (*Act 1*).

Although the Mayor's refusal of Claire's offer, at the end of Act 1, allows Ill time to come to terms with the accusation, it constitutes a turning point in Ill's characterisation. As the town has appeared to have disassociated itself with the prospect of abundant wealth, Ill is no longer the person on whom all hopes are pinned. Humanity seems to prevail now: 'DER BÜRGERMEISTER [...] Im Namen der Menschlichkeit. Lieber bleiben wir arm denn blutbefleckt' (*Act 1*).

Act 2 will reveal that Ill will eventually be reinstated as the person on whom all hopes are pinned. The context of this status, however, will be altogether more sinister, as hope will be pinned on his death.

Ill as a hunted man

Ill soon has to concede that both time and money are against him, as he begins to feel hunted ('gejagt'). In Act 1 he was very much a part of the group and at the start of Act 2 he still believes that the whole town is backing him, although this proves to be an illusion. Just as he deluded himself into believing that his youth excused his behaviour with Klara, he now pretends that his wife and children, who are keen to avoid breakfasting with him, are good and loyal family members.

> **Key quotation**
>
> ILL Kommt die Mutter zum Frühstück?
> DIE TOCHTER Sie bleibe oben. Sie sei müde.
> ILL Eine gute Mutter habt ihr, Kinder. [...]
> ILL Du willst nicht mit uns essen, Karl? [...]
> DIE TOCHTER *steht auf* Ich gehe auch, Vater. [...]
> ILL *gerührt, niest in sein Taschentuch* Gute Kinder, brave Kinder.
> (*Act 2*)

The citizens feign solidarity with Ill but he soon observes that their spending patterns are altering. Their enthusiastic purchasing on credit and obsequious compliments to him imply a hidden agenda which isolates him from everyone else. Initially, he chooses to merely admonish himself for being an old sinner, acknowledging that he should not have played his 'youthful trick' ('Jugendstreich') on Klara. At the same time, he convinces himself that the support shown to him by the townsfolk proves that she has miscalculated.

The pressure increases as the debts amass, and Ill begins to realise that the yellow shoes which all the citizens are wearing, bought on credit, represent the collective's solidarity against him. The people have been corrupted and have succumbed to consumerism. Ill's initial response to the deceit of his fellow citizens is a physical one: he throws the consumer goods at them.

At this point in the play, the audience is informed that the black panther has escaped and must be hunted down. Ill's sense of unease turns into an animalistic fear which leaves him trembling and demanding Claire's arrest. The threat increases, as he realises that he has no support from the Police Officer or the Mayor.

> **Key quotation**
>
> DER POLIZIST [...] Ich trage schließlich auch neue Schuhe. *Er zeigt seine Füße.*
> ILL Auch Sie.
> DER POLIZIST Sehn Sie.
> (Act 2)

Ill feels that the townsfolk's determination to capture the panther reflects their pursuit of him. This is shown further during the chase, as the citizens change their interpretation of Ill's past behaviour from youthful self-interest to criminal perjury.

> **Key quotation**
>
> DER BÜRGERMEISTER Daß wir den Vorschlag der Dame verurteilen, bedeutet nicht, daß wir die Verbrechen billigen, die zu diesem Vorschlag geführt haben. Für den Posten eines Bürgermeisters sind gewisse Forderungen sittlicher Natur zu stellen, die Sie nicht mehr erfüllen, das müssen Sie einsehen.
> (Act 2)

By the time that Ill goes to the station to escape, he knows that he is lost. Surrounded by the citizens, he covers his face, acknowledging guilt and humiliation. He says that someone will stop him from leaving the town: '[...] Einer wird mich zurückhalten' (*Act 2*). That someone is himself. He knows that if he flees, Claire will hunt him down and he knows that, as a guilty man, he must now accept his fate. This is a second turning point in the characterisation of Ill.

Ill as a tragic hero

In Act 3, Alfred Ill is a changed man. He has undergone **catharsis**, recognising his guilt and becoming free of his previous fear. He recognises that his customers despise

> **catharsis** *die Katharsis* the process of releasing, and thereby providing relief from, strong or repressed emotions

him and he has ceased to fight against the threat of death. Having hidden in his room for several days, he emerges in old, tattered clothes, which contrast with the citizens' affluence. He sells his goods to his prospective murderers in a friendly manner and does not want to struggle. He accepts death as atonement ('Buße') for the sins of the past.

Key quotation

ILL [...] Alles ist meine Tat, die Eunuchen, der Butler, der Sarg, die Milliarde. Ich kann mir nicht mehr helfen und auch euch nicht mehr.
(Act 3)

He refuses to spare the citizens the act of murdering him and does not accept the Mayor's suggestion that he should commit suicide. In the car journey that he takes with his family, he sees his life pass before him. He recognises that his wife has long since abandoned him. He goes calmly to his death, one brave individual who has restored order in his own self. He becomes a tragic hero, having acknowledged his guilt.

Aufgabe 1

Ill ist die einzige Figur, mit der im Verlauf des Dramas eine innere Veränderung vor sich geht. Was für ein Mensch ist Ill?

Sehen Sie die vier untenstehenden Phasen seines Lebens sowie die Liste von Adjektiven an. Entscheiden Sie, welche Adjektive seinen Charakter und Geisteszustand in jeder Phase am besten beschreiben.

a. Ill als junger Mann und seine Beziehung zu Klara

b. Ill als angesehener Mensch in der Güllener Gesellschaft

c. Ills Reaktion auf die Rückkehr der alten Dame

d. Ills Reaktion auf Claires Forderung

zärtlich	aufgeblasen	beunruhigt
zusammengebrochen	egoistisch	anständig
unehrlich	beklommen	gefasst
selbstsicher	hitzig	überängstlich
stutzig	manipulativ	aufgeklärt
selbstzufrieden	gewieft	bang
schmeichlerisch	betrügerisch	

Aufgabe 2

Wählen Sie nun einen Güllener Bürger aus. Schreiben Sie einen Nachruf (‚epitaph')
auf Alfred Ill, in dem Sie beschreiben, wie sein Tod Ihr Leben beeinflusst hat.

- Vermissen Sie ihn?

- Wie geht es Ihnen seit seinem Tod?

- Wie hat sich das Leben in Güllen seit Ills Tod verändert?

Claire Zachanassian/Klara Wäscher

As the old lady who pays the community of Güllen the visit and offers a billion in
exchange for a life, Claire Zachanassian is the embodiment of the power of money.
Unlike Alfred Ill, whose character undergoes a development, her character remains
static throughout the story. Any developments have happened before the play even
begins and are reflected in her two different names.

Her original name of Klara Wäscher has symbolic meaning: 'Klara' means 'clear' or 'pure'
in German, and 'waschen' means 'to wash/cleanse'. It also suggests 'washerwoman' or
even 'scrubber', with associations of working-class background.

Claire's backstory

Claire was born in Güllen and, although the audience only meets her as an older
woman, Ill supplies information about what she looked like as a young girl: '[...] sie
[...] ging, mit wehenden roten Haaren, biegsam, gertenschlank, zart, eine
verteufelt schöne Hexe' (*Act 1*).

The image of wavy flame-red hair communicates a vitality which is echoed in later
references to how the young Klara behaved. She was the daughter of Gottfried
Wäscher, who is referred to in the story as the 'architect' of a public toilet on Güllen's
station platform. Klara's mother fled from her drunken husband and Gottfried died in
1911 in an asylum, a year after Klara had left the town. At school, Klara was beaten
by the teachers because of bad marks and bad behaviour, achieving satisfactory
results only in botany and zoology. In her youth she liked playing pranks on people,
often together with Ill. One of these pranks involved stealing potatoes. In Act 1 of the
play, Ill and the Mayor refer to this episode while composing a welcome speech that
will ingratiate themselves into her favour. Their aim is to portray her character as
charitable from a very early age onwards.

Claire herself, however, dispels the notion of her benevolence by explaining that the
theft of the potatoes was simply a bribe so that she and Ill could make love in a bed
rather than in the woods.

Ill gets to know Klara when she is 17 and he is 20. Klara becomes pregnant by Ill but he does not want to accept responsibility. Klara files a paternity suit ('die Vaterschaftsklage') but Ill bribes witnesses to state that Klara had been promiscuous with them. Klara therefore loses the case, is socially shunned and the court judgement forces her to leave Güllen.

The audience is told that she left the town a forlorn red-haired girl, at whom the townsfolk jeered. Initially, she becomes a prostitute in Hamburg. Her daughter Geneviève is taken from her at birth by a Christian welfare group and only survives for a year. In a Hamburg brothel she gets to know her first husband, 'den alten Zachanassian mit seinen Milliarden aus Armenien' *(Act 1)*, and inherits his entire fortune (three billion) when he dies. With this legacy, 'Claire Zachanassian' is now able to realise her girlhood plan of returning to her village for justice. She has never forgotten the lies that Ill told about her in court and wants to set the record straight for herself: 'Das Leben ging weiter, aber ich habe nichts vergessen, Ill' *(Act 1)*.

Symbolically, her new surname is a combination of the surnames of the world's most successful entrepreneurs: Zacharoff (an arms dealer and industrialist), Onassis (a shipping magnate) and Gulbenkian (an oil baron).

Before returning to Güllen, Claire marries six other men: Graf Holk, a foreign minister; a fashion designer; a surgeon; the owner of Western Railways; Lord Ismael; and Pedro, the owner of a tobacco plantation. All the marriages are short-lived and inconsequential to Claire, although she enjoys the short-term fame that each association brings.

Before the play begins, Claire – as is revealed later in the play – has also managed to purchase all of Güllen's industry and has then systematically ruined it. At the same time, she has supported neighbouring communities as a philanthropist, someone who donates generously to promote the welfare of others, in this case by founding a nursery and supporting the construction of a new church.

Claire during the play

The play starts with Claire's return to Güllen after a 45-year absence. She is given a bizarre appearance at the beginning of the play.

Key quotation

Von rechts kommt Claire Zachanassian, zweiundsechzig, rothaarig, Perlenhalsband, riesige goldene Armringe, aufgedonnert, unmöglich, aber gerade darum wieder eine Dame von Welt, mit einer seltsamen Grazie, trotz allem Grotesken.
(Act 1)

Her physical appearance conveys her eccentric personality, as well as her extreme wealth. The red hair mirrors the vibrantly attractive mane of her youth. She is adorned with pearls and gold, communicating her desire to show the world her buying power. Claire survived a car crash in which she lost a left leg, and a plane crash, when she lost her right arm and hand. She now has prosthetic limbs. Her artificial limbs are a metaphor for her interpretation of morality; she is cold and inhumane.

Key quotation

ILL *läßt entsetzt ihre Hand fahren* Klara, ist denn überhaupt alles Prothese an dir!

CLAIRE ZACHANASSIAN Fast.
(Act 1)

When Claire returns to her impoverished home town with an entourage of peculiar men and an offer of great wealth, the citizens are expecting a benevolent donator. However, Claire links her donation to a condition: namely that the town should agree to support her in her quest for justice. They discover that Alfred Ill, the town's main retailer, must be killed because he lied about his relationship with Klara.

Claire uses the town, which turned a blind eye to Klara's suffering as a young girl, as a tool to exact her revenge. She has waited a lifetime to return ('Das habe ich mir immer vorgenommen. Mein Leben lang, seit ich Güllen verlassen habe' (*Act 1*)) and now waits for the town to accept her offer, confident in the power of her own wealth: 'Ich warte' (*Act 1*).

Claire as a superhuman figure

When Claire arrives on the 'Rasende Roland' train (the express train that never stops in Güllen but which does on the occasion of her visit), Dürrenmatt's audience and the townspeople witness a supernatural ('übernatürlich') occurrence: 'Die Naturgesetze sind aufgehoben' (*Act 1*).

The idea that Claire is a superhuman force is reiterated in many different contexts throughout the play. As she sweeps off the train in her black apparel, the Teacher describes her as an awful figure, resembling the Greek goddess of fate, Clotho, who takes control of the lives of others: 'Sollte Klotho heißen, nicht Claire, der traut man es noch zu, daß sie Lebensfäden spinnt' (*Act 1*).

This sense of threat and imminent catastrophe is reinforced when Claire talks with Ill about their past and present lives. He wants her to believe that he is financially ruined and that his life has been hell since she left. She wants him to know that she has money and has become hell itself. She infers that she has become what she is, a hellish force, because of the hell she endured at Ill's and others' hands.

> **Key quotation**
>
> ILL Ich lebe in einer Hölle, seit du von mir gegangen bist.
> CLAIRE ZACHANASSIAN Und ich bin die Hölle geworden.
> *(Act 1)*

Claire herself informs the citizens that she cannot be destroyed ('Bin nicht umzubringen' (*Act 1*)), and Dürrenmatt's choice of the balcony of the hotel 'Zum Goldenen Apostel' as her place to watch over the town reinforces the notion that she is a supernatural being who looks down on mankind and comments on people's weaknesses.

At the end of the play, she is referred to in the stage directions as a motionless stone idol as she departs from the town: *'Aus dem Hintergrund kommt Claire Zachanassian in ihrer Sänfte, unbeweglich, ein altes Götzenbild aus Stein* [...]' (*Act 3*).

This image of a cold, inanimate statue correlates with her timelessness, as well as with her physical artificiality. Her appearance mirrors the image of Ill, who will be preserved in a stone mausoleum in Capri. In death, he has returned to Claire who is, herself, as cold as death.

Claire, from a stylised production in 2014 at the Deutsches Theater, Berlin

Claire as a dehumanising figure

Ill refers to Claire sycophantically as 'unchanged' ('Doch d u bist die gleiche geblieben' (*Act 1*)), yet the references to Claire's physical artificiality make her a grotesque parody of the beautiful, red-haired, willowy girl whom Ill wronged.

Life experiences (the accidents which have robbed her of some of her limbs, as well as the moral and spiritual torment of Ill's denial of her and of being forced into prostitution) have had a profound and embittering effect upon Claire. Her habit of giving each of her husbands (except her first one) and her employees a series of rhyming nicknames demonstrates her contempt and condescension towards her fellow human beings.

The process of stripping men of their names is a form of revenge on the sex that stripped her of her own dignity. The deprecation is almost exclusively reserved for men, although she does mock the girl who was top of the class at school, who is now the Mayor's wife ('*betrachtet die Gattin durch ihr Lorgnon* Annettchen Dummermuth, unsere Klassenerste' (*Act 1*)), and clearly thinks very little of Ill's wife: '*Mathildchen Blumhard. Erinnere mich, wie du hinter der Ladentüre auf Alfred lauertest. Mager bist du geworden und bleich* [...]' (*Act 1*). Her use of diminutives of their names underlines Claire's contempt for both women.

The most powerful example of Claire's dehumanising treatment of others comes in the form of the two men she had blinded and castrated for lying about her in court. Stripped of their sight, their manhood and their identity, they were made to join her entourage of nameless men.

Key quotation

CLAIRE ZACHANASSIAN Erzählt nun, was ich mit euch getan habe, Koby und Loby.

[...]

DIE BEIDEN Kastriert und geblendet. Kastriert und geblendet.
(*Act 1*)

Aufgabe 3

a. Übersetzen Sie das untenstehende Zitat, das sich mit Claires Ansicht über die Menschlichkeit befasst, ins Englische:

 Die Menschlichkeit, meine Herren, ist für die Börse der Millionäre geschaffen, mit meiner Finanzkraft leistet man sich eine Weltordnung. Die Welt machte mich zu einer Hure, nun mache ich sie zu einem Bordell. Wer nicht blechen* kann, muß hinhalten**, will er mittanzen. Ihr wollt mittanzen. Anständig ist nur, wer zahlt, und ich zahle. Güllen für einen Mord, Konjunktur für eine Leiche.
(*Act 3*)

* **blechen** to pay up   ** **hinhalten** to stall or hold out

b. Welche Adjektive würden Sie benutzen, um die alte Dame in dieser Szene des Stücks zu beschreiben?

Claire as a human figure

Despite Claire's relentless pursuit of 'justice' and revenge, she is not the embodiment of justice. She knows that, as the world's richest woman, she can buy everything and everyone. However, it is possible to interpret her campaign as an attempt to bring back a lost time of happiness. For this reason, she instructs her sedan-carriers to take her to the two rural locations where she encountered love: the barn and the forest. In these locations, her language changes from brief, functional utterances into nostalgic reminiscences on the time she spent with Ill. In Act 3, the Teacher attempts to appeal to her sense of humanity: 'Frau Zachanassian! Sie sind ein verletztes liebendes Weib' (*Act 3*).

In the setting of the barn and the woods, Claire does indeed seek to recall the past because she was happy then. During these conversations, it seems as if the present no longer matters. Yet, despite the love that she felt for Ill, she believes that she can only salvage the past, and make the dreams of her youth a reality once more, by destroying Ill.

Key quotation

CLAIRE ZACHANASSIAN Ich liebte dich. Du hast mich verraten. Doch der Traum von Leben, von Liebe, von Vertrauen, diesen wirklichen Traum habe ich nicht vergessen. Ich will ihn wieder errichten mit meinen Milliarden, die Vergangenheit ändern, indem ich dich vernichte.
(*Act 3*)

Aufgabe 4

a. Definieren Sie die untenstehenden Begriffe, die mögliche Motive darstellen, auf Deutsch.

Gerechtigkeit	Liebe	Rache
Schuld	Gier	Verrat

b. Schauen Sie sich nochmals die Motive oben an. Was motiviert Claire Zachanassian am stärksten? Kann man ihre Handlungen Ihrer Meinung nach rechtfertigen? Warum (nicht)?

Aufgabe 5

Sie haben den Auftrag bekommen, ein Prequel zum Theaterstück zu verfassen, das Claires Handlungen im Stück rechtfertigt. Stellen Sie sich vor, wie Claires Leben vor ihrer Ankunft in Güllen war. Wählen Sie eine Schlüsselszene aus ihrem Leben aus, die die Handlung des Stücks beeinflusst. Schreiben Sie die Szene mit Regieanweisungen auf. Sie können dabei wie Dürrenmatt Inschriften oder Plakate benutzen, um die Situation zu beschreiben. Zum Beispiel: ‚Alfred Ill leugnet, Claire geschwängert zu haben!' Finden Sie auch ein passendes Zitat im Stück, das die Bedeutung dieses Augenblicks für Claire unterstreicht.

Tips for assessment

When critically evaluating a character in your exam, you will have to present points of view using evidence from the work. You might wish to link what you learn about the character to the themes of the play, or to show how the character's behaviour affects others or impacts on the plot. Never simply describe a character, but ensure that you also analyse them, thinking about the wider context of the play as you do so.

Minor characters

The effectiveness of this tragicomedy depends not only on the individual minor characters ('Nebenfiguren') but also their collective significance, particularly the group of citizens of Güllen ('the Visited'), and Claire's entourage ('the Visitors').

There are various groups of minor characters who interconnect and influence the protagonists' characters, in particular Ill's character development.

Families of the protagonists

Claire's parents are already dead but her father is brought to life when his architectural contribution to Güllen in the past is overstated in the town's welcoming speech. On the one hand, Claire and Ill's illegitimate daughter Geneviève is a secret of the protagonists' past but, on the other hand, her early death is an allusion to her father's death at the end of the play. Rather than choosing the rather poor Claire and their future daughter, Ill favours prosperity and status by marrying Mathilde Blumhard, the shopkeeper's daughter. Their two children Ottilie and Karl, portrayed as having no direction in their lives to start with, embrace the newly-rich lifestyle fully, just like their mother, and they become the antithesis of Ill by the end of the play.

> **Key quotation**
>
> ILL Morgens früh, nicht wahr? Statt aufs Arbeitsamt zu gehen?
> DIE TOCHTER Alle spielen Tennis von meinen Freundinnen. [...]
> ILL Ich habe dich in einem Wagen gesehen, Karl [...]
> DER SOHN Nur ein Opel Olympia, die sind nicht so teuer.
> ILL Wann lerntest du fahren?
> *Schweigen.*
> ILL Statt Arbeit zu suchen [...]
> DER SOHN Manchmal. [...]
> ILL [...] Dabei fand ich einen Pelzmantel.
> FRAU ILL Zur Ansicht.
> *(Act 3)*

Enjoying the lifestyle, they justify their actions, purchases and the consequent debts by the need to keep up with their fellow citizens. At the same time, they also hide behind their strong belief that nothing is going to happen, and that Claire's request is just a bad joke. As three representatives of the newly-rich town, Dürrenmatt portrays them as despicably weak, enjoying a trip to the cinema while their father and husband is killed by their fellow citizens to fulfil Claire's deal. Ill's death secures his family's continued prosperity.

Aufgabe 6

Lesen Sie die verschiedenen Szenen, in denen Ills Familienmitglieder mit ihm sprechen, noch einmal. Welche Sprache verwenden sie, um ihre Handlungen Ill gegenüber zu rechtfertigen? Mit welchen Worten versuchen sie, Ill zu beruhigen?

The Visited ('die Besuchten')

The weak humans, portrayed by the townspeople, are often referred to as 'the Visited' when analysing the character relationships in *Der Besuch der alten Dame*. While all the townspeople are potential beneficiaries of Claire's billion and therefore Ill's death, five minor characters have important functions among the group of 'Visited', namely the Mayor, Doctor, Teacher, Priest and Police Officer.

The Mayor and Police Officer

The Mayor represents the town's authority and political power. The Police Officer is the executor of the political administration. He is also the guardian of safety in the town and, therefore, he reneges on his professional responsibilities and oath through his behaviour during the play. The audience might chuckle when the old lady asks him to ignore criminal activities, but when the Police Officer follows this request in Act 2, it is clear that Ill is no longer safe. In the end, it is the Police Officer who excuses the murder of Ill by characterising him as a pig instead of a human being, just minutes before Ill's death: 'Steh auf, du Schwein' (*Act 3*). The Mayor, on the other hand, maintains a two-faced nature throughout the play. At the beginning, he whitewashes Claire's past actions and promises Ill the role of mayor. His insincerity reaches a peak when he votes for justice and against criminal actions. By behaving in this way, he condones Ill's death but disguises his own treachery by celebrating Ill as the reason for the Claire Zachanassian Foundation.

The Doctor and the Teacher

The Doctor is a representative of social and health care but also the character who pronounces people's death. While he is initially shocked by the old lady's request for him to lie on future death certificates, the Doctor not only proceeds to follow her instructions, but also benefits from the rising prosperity in the town: by the end of the play, his old car has been upgraded to a Mercedes. His weakness is also visible at the beginning of Act 3, when he lets the Teacher speak up and make pleas for the townspeople and their debts. When Claire makes clear to the two honourable men that they will only get her money if Ill dies, the Doctor's helplessness is emphasised by his cry: 'Mein Gott, was sollen wir tun?' (*Act 3*).

This particular scene shows the Teacher, as so often in the play, attempting to rescue Ill from his ultimate fate and to prevent the townspeople from committing a crime. As a representative of **humanism**, he is also the moral authority of Güllen. His strong beliefs and values force him to speak up. However, it is he who, together with the Mayor, leads the final assembly, misusing these values and ideals to legitimise the murder of Ill: 'Mit unseren Idealen müssen wir nun eben in Gottes Namen Ernst machen, blutigen Ernst' (*Act 3*). Humanist values have capitulated to self-interest.

> **humanism** *der Humanismus* a non-religious belief system which uses reason and ethics to inform decisions about human welfare and how best to live

The Priest

The Priest represents Christian values but is also the representative of the Church as an institution. Although he epitomises the Christian values of dignity, humility and peacefulness, he carries a rifle by Act 2 and is driven, like his fellow citizens, by the promised prosperity when he buys a new church bell on credit.

Key quotation

ILL Eine zweite Glocke?
DER PFARRER Der Ton ist hervorragend. Nicht? Voll und kräftig. Positiv, nur positiv.
ILL *schreit auf* Auch Sie, Pfarrer! Auch Sie!
(*Act 2*)

Prior to this, the Priest insists that Ill only need fear God and protect his mortal soul. Nevertheless, he is engaged in the same subversive behaviour as the other citizens, which threatens Ill's physical safety. There are two moments when the Priest breaks free of this hypocrisy: firstly, when he urges Ill to flee and, secondly, when Ill asks him not to pray for him but for the citizens of Güllen and the Priest responds with a plea to God for himself and his fellow townspeople: 'Gott sei uns gnädig' (*Act 3*).

The Priest's lines in the concluding chorus, however, demonstrate that his reflectiveness is rather short-lived: 'Es berstet an Weihnachten, Ostern und Pfingsten / Vom Andrang der Christen das Münster' (*Act 3*). He and his institution seem satisfied that the house of prayer is full at special Christian events like Easter and Christmas, rather than encouraging regular weekly attendance.

Aufgabe 7

Wählen Sie eine der fünf Nebenfiguren aus. Analysieren Sie, wie sich diese Figur gegenüber Ill verhält. Wie und wann verändert sich die Beziehung zu Ill? Woran kann das Publikum das erkennen? Gibt es außer sprachlichen Merkmalen sonstige Zeichen (zum Beispiel bestimmte Requisiten)?

The Visitors ('die Besucher')

The group of visitors consists of Claire Zachanassian's entourage: the witnesses of the past, as well as Claire's last three husbands. All of these minor characters share the role of serving the old lady. They are dependent on her and her wealth and emphasise the comical awkwardness of their mistress' appearance ('Erscheinung ihrer Herrin'). Three of them, the butler Boby and the two eunuchs Koby and Toby, are of particular importance as they bring Claire's offer and request to life. As witnesses of the past, they confirm Ill's betrayal of Klara Wäscher in the courts of Güllen 45 years

Claire's idiosyncratic entourage of 'Visitors' accompanies her throughout her time in Güllen

ago: Boby was the former judge of Güllen who acquitted Ill of his charges, and Koby (Jakob Hühnelein) and Toby (Ludwig Sparr) were bribed by Ill in order to claim (wrongly) under oath that they too had had sex with Klara.

These three characters are also a constant reminder that, with money, one can buy and do everything, even getting people castrated or blinded without any legal consequences. Dürrenmatt challenges his audience via the figures of the two eunuchs; through these characters he questions whether human beings really are their own individual selves with their own identity.

Aufgabe 8

Schreiben Sie einen kurzen Text über die beiden Eunuchen. Inwieweit sind die beiden Eunuchen ein komisches Element dieser Tragikomödie?

> DER POLIZIST *mißtrauisch* Ihr scheint Erfahrungen mit der Polizei gemacht zu haben, ihr kleinen dicken Männer.
> DIE BEIDEN *staunend* Männer, er hält uns für Männer!
> DER POLIZIST Was seid ihr denn sonst, zum Teufel!
> DIE BEIDEN Werden's schon merken, werden's schon merken!
> (Act 1)

Furthermore, Dürrenmatt wonders whether all human beings are, in actual fact, weak and fallible, as the townspeople appear to be by the end of the play. With Ill's death, Claire's dream is fulfilled and the witnesses from the past are no longer needed.

Reunited with Ill's body, the old lady and the visitors depart, and leave the people of Güllen to their prosperity and their potential moral conflict, although it would appear that the citizens have no qualms about the murder at the end.

Aufgabe 9

Da Sie sich nun im Detail mit den Nebenfiguren beschäftigt haben, sehen Sie sich die Abbildung der Figurenkonstellation an (**Character map**, S. 67). Beachten Sie dabei, dass einige Nebenfiguren Ill in ihrer Jugend näher waren, aber jetzt im Dienst der alten Dame stehen. Erklären Sie auf Deutsch, wie die verschiedenen Nebenfiguren mit den Hauptfiguren in Verbindung stehen.

Einige Fragen, die Ihnen bei der Analyse helfen:

- Was erfahren wir über die Nebenfigur?
- Wie beschreibt Dürrenmatt die Person?
- In welcher Beziehung steht Claire/Ill zu dieser Nebenfigur?
- Welche Rolle spielt die Nebenfigur für Claire/Ill?
- Welche Rolle spielt die Nebenfigur für die Tragikomödie?
- Wie beeinflusst die Nebenfigur den Handlungsablauf?
- Inwiefern handelt diese Nebenfigur allein oder in einer Gruppe?

Achten Sie auch auf die Hinweise in den beiden Upgrade-Kästchen.

Writing about character

When writing about a character you could consider the following aspects:

- the character's physical appearance ('die äußere Erscheinung der Figur')
- the character's social status ('der soziale Status der Figur')
- the character's visible behaviour ('das sichtbare Verhalten der Figur')
- the character's psychological motivations ('die psychischen Beweggründe der Figur')
- the character's emotional and social relationships ('die emotionalen und sozialen Beziehungen der Figur')
- how the character's behaviour affects the people around them ('wie sich das Verhalten der Figur auf ihr Umfeld auswirkt')

Ensure that you refer back to the text and support your arguments with quotations. For example:

The Teacher's social and moral authority over Güllen and its citizens makes him eager to open his fellow citizens' eyes early on in the play. They subsequently disappoint him: 'Güllener. Ich bin euer alter Lehrer [...] Ich will die Wahrheit verkünden, auch wenn unsere Armut ewig währen sollte' (*Act 3*).

Once Claire's deal is known, the Mayor begins to plan ahead on how to spend the 500 million for the town, including a new town hall. This affects Ill directly. Ill realises that they expect his death: 'Ihr habt mich schon zum Tode verurteilt' (*Act 2*).

Useful phrases

Die Stagnation der Figur von ... The stagnation of the character of ...

Die Veränderung/Entwicklung der Hauptfigur im Laufe des Theaterstücks zeigt ...
The change/development of the main character during the course of the play shows ...

Im Gegenteil zur Protagonistin verändert sich die männliche Hauptfigur ... In contrast to the (female) main character, the male main character changes ...

Die Nebenfigur ist ein Symbol für ... The minor character is a symbol of ...

... steht stellvertretend für Ills Vergangenheit. ... is representative of Ill's past.

Nebenfiguren repräsentieren neue/andere Perspektiven, die wir durch die Hauptfiguren sonst nicht gewonnen hätten. Minor characters represent new/different perspectives, which we would otherwise not have gained from the main characters.

In diesem Theaterstück versucht der Schriftsteller den Eindruck zu erwecken, dass ... In this play the playwright seeks to convey the impression that ...

Eine wichtige Funktion dieser Figur ist ... An important function/role of this character is ...

Ein Schlüsselelement dieses Charakters ist, dass ... A key element of this character is that ...

Ein Beispiel, das diesen Gedanken bestätigt, ist ... An example that confirms this thought is ...

Außerdem ist zu beachten, dass ... Moreover, it is worth noting that ...

Vocabulary

beschreiben to describe

die Beschreibung description

die Charaktereigenschaften (fpl) characteristics

charakterisieren to characterise

darstellen to portray

deutlich machen to reveal

dramatische Elemente (npl) dramatic elements

die Eigenschaften (fpl) features

enthüllen to disclose

erkennen lassen to reveal

die Figuren des (Theater-)Stücks/des Dramas/der Tragikomödie (fpl) the characters of the play/drama/tragicomedy

die Hauptfigur the main character

ein Hinweis sein für to be an indication for

auf Kleinigkeiten achten to pay attention to detail

komische Elemente (npl) comic elements

mitteilen to disclose

die Nebenfigur the minor character

der Protagonist/die Protagonistin the main character

repräsentieren to represent

vertreten to represent

Character map

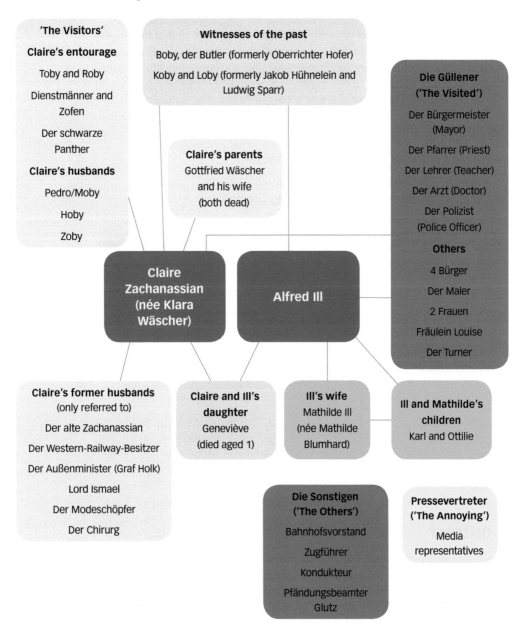

'The Visitors'

Claire's entourage

Toby and Roby

Dienstmänner and Zofen

Der schwarze Panther

Claire's husbands

Pedro/Moby

Hoby

Zoby

Witnesses of the past

Boby, der Butler (formerly Oberrichter Hofer)

Koby and Loby (formerly Jakob Hühnelein and Ludwig Sparr)

Claire's parents
Gottfried Wäscher and his wife (both dead)

Die Güllener ('The Visited')

Der Bürgermeister (Mayor)

Der Pfarrer (Priest)

Der Lehrer (Teacher)

Der Arzt (Doctor)

Der Polizist (Police Officer)

Others

4 Bürger

Der Maler

2 Frauen

Fräulein Louise

Der Turner

Claire Zachanassian (née Klara Wäscher)

Alfred Ill

Claire's former husbands
(only referred to)

Der alte Zachanassian

Der Western-Railway-Besitzer

Der Außenminister (Graf Holk)

Lord Ismael

Der Modeschöpfer

Der Chirurg

Claire and Ill's daughter
Geneviève (died aged 1)

Ill's wife
Mathilde Ill (née Mathilde Blumhard)

Ill and Mathilde's children
Karl and Ottilie

Die Sonstigen ('The Others')

Bahnhofsvorstand

Zugführer

Kondukteur

Pfändungsbeamter Glutz

Pressevertreter ('The Annoying')

Media representatives

Language

Friedrich Dürrenmatt's language choices play an important part in the alienation effect ('Verfremdungseffekt') discussed on page 47. The playwright wants the audience to remain detached from the characters he presents so that they may become more aware of the chaotic and unpredictable nature of the world. Language is shown to be a means of ambiguity and deception: self-deception, the deception of others and the deception of the audience. Dürrenmatt creates an illusory world ('eine Scheinwelt') in which what is said is frequently not what is meant.

Dialogue

In the play, Dürrenmatt uses three forms of dialogue:

- talking to each other – Ill and Claire in the forest or barn
- talking past each other – Ill and the citizens of Güllen
- talking alongside each other – the chorus of citizens.

Aufgabe 1

Warum hat Dürrenmatt diese drei Formen des Dialogs verwendet? Was will er mit ihnen erreichen? Für wie effektiv halten Sie diese Formen?

Key quotation

ILL Ich bin verzweifelt. Ich bin zu allem fähig. Ich warne dich, Klara. [...] wenn du jetzt nicht sagst, daß alles nur ein Spaß ist, ein grausamer Spaß. *Er richtet das Gewehr auf sie.*

CLAIRE ZACHANASSIAN Und du gingst nicht weiter, unten auf der Straße. Du starrtest zu mir herauf, fast finster, fast böse, als wolltest du mir ein Leid antun, und dennoch waren deine Augen voll Liebe.

Ill läßt das Gewehr sinken.
(Act 2)

Contrast

The plain-speaking language used by Claire contrasts markedly with the sycophantic ('kriecherisch') nd insincere words of the townspeople, including her former lover Alfred Ill. Claire, as the world's richest woman, has all the material goods that she wants and can therefore afford to speak candidly and honestly, whereas the townsfolk desire the wealth that she has bestowed on neighbouring villages and are prepared to speak and behave obsequiously ('unterwürfig') to obtain it.

Even before Claire arrives at the station, the Mayor is planning a euphemistic speech of welcome which praises 'strengths' that the young Klara might not really have had, omitting early encounters that she had with the police.

> **Key quotation**
>
> ILL Da kann ich dem Bürgermeister dienen. Klara liebte die Gerechtigkeit. Ausgesprochen. Einmal wurde ein Vagabund abgeführt. Sie bewarf den Polizisten mit Steinen.
>
> DER BÜRGERMEISTER Gerechtigkeitsliebe. Nicht schlecht. Wirkt immer. Aber die Geschichte mit dem Polizisten unterschlagen wir besser.
> *(Act 1)*

The Mayor's selective use of the truth differs strikingly from the way in which Claire herself speaks to the train driver who has objected in a pompous manner to her pulling the emergency brake:

> **Key quotation**
>
> DER ZUGFÜHRER Ich warte auf eine Erklärung. Dienstlich. Im Namen der Eisenbahndirektion.
>
> CLAIRE ZACHANASSIAN Sie sind ein Schafskopf. Ich will eben das Städtchen mal besuchen. Soll ich etwa aus Ihrem Schnellzug springen?
> *(Act 1)*

The fawning, ingratiating words used by Ill to describe Claire's appearance ('Mein Zauberhexchen' *(Act 1)*) contrast with the candid observations offered by Claire about Ill: 'Unsinn. Du bist fett geworden. Und grau und versoffen' *(Act 1)*.

She has nothing to lose by speaking the truth, whereas he has everything to lose, should she take offence. Claire continues to speak the truth and the town officials continue to use the truth selectively. By the end of Act 1, the Mayor welcomes her with a series of obsequious and misinformed blunders which are corrected by Ill, then changed into diplomatic untruths, which Claire corrects:

> **Key quotation**
>
> DER BÜRGERMEISTER [...] Hatte doch unser Kläri einer armen alten Witwe Nahrung verschafft [...]
>
> CLAIRE ZACHANASSIAN [...] die Kartoffeln für die Witwe Boll habe ich gestohlen [...]
> *(Act 1)*

Dürrenmatt's ironic contrasting of the hypocrisy of the Güllen citizens' language with the cold, objective frankness of the old lady provides an important source of black humour in the play.

Further contrasts can be seen when comparing the emotional language Ill uses to communicate his increasing panic over the citizens' changing attitude to Claire's offer with the cool, objective utterances which Claire makes about her financial affairs. She is manoeuvring her finances in readiness for remarrying and delivering the cheque, while he is witnessing the town preparing for the same event. She can simultaneously reflect on her love affair, when she would ward off the grinning advances of two other boys so that she could sleep with Ill, and transfer a billion to her current account in readiness for when he is killed. The link is clear: Claire sells some shares to fund her cheque, while the citizens buy expensive goods on credit, which the cheque will ultimately pay for.

> **Key quotation**
>
> CLAIRE ZACHANASSIAN Laß die Dupont-Aktien aufkaufen, Boby.
>
> ILL Kognak kaufte Helmesberger bei mir. Dabei verdient er seit Jahren nicht und lebt von der Suppenanstalt.
> *(Act 2)*

Ill tries to tell the Mayor that his new town hall plan is Ill's death sentence, while Claire plans to bring the rich and famous to her lavish wedding.

> **Key quotation**
>
> ILL Ihr habt mich schon zum Tode verurteilt.
>
> DER BÜRGERMEISTER Herr Ill!
>
> Ill *leise* Der Plan beweist es! Beweist es!
>
> CLAIRE ZACHANASSIAN Onassis kommt. Der Herzog und die Herzogin. Aga.
> *(Act 2)*

The play demonstrates further use of contrast in the dilapidation ('Verkommenheit') of the town at the start and its self-confidence at the end; in the Teacher's defence of Western values and the actual behaviour of the citizens; and in the depiction of the press, the function of which is the truthful reporting of events but which conceals the truth behind the events surrounding Ill's death.

Repetition and sentence construction

Just as Claire's language distinguishes itself from that of the other characters by its honesty, so too it differs from the language of the townspeople and Claire's entourage in its lack of repetition or duplication ('Verdoppelung'). The chorus of townsfolk repeats and chants, particularly in Act 2, and this pattern of speech reinforces a number of characteristics of the collective: that they are united in their new-found, borrowed wealth ('Wir ließen's aufschreiben, Herr Ill, wir ließen's aufschreiben' (*Act 2*)); and that their collective status can be threatening, once Ill has been ostracised.

> **Key quotation**
>
> DER BÜRGERMEISTER Wir begleiten Sie!
>
> DER ERSTE Wir begleiten Sie!
>
> DER ZWEITE Wir begleiten Sie!
>
> (*Act 2*)

With the use of repetition, Dürrenmatt also emphasises what the citizens are doing, leaving the audience with no illusion about what is going on. By the end of Act 2, the level of imbecilic repetition has escalated, proving that they are morally and linguistically impaired. The thought processes of the townsfolk have, like their language, been castrated; they are spiritually emasculated and blind to their actions and guilt.

The repetition of the Güllen choruses mirrors the style of speech attributed to the two eunuchs Koby and Loby. Just as the repeated lines of the chorus reinforce the mindless following of the crowd, so the two blind men demonstrate their infantile state which has been caused by the sins of their youth. When they arrive in Güllen, they chant, 'Wir sind in Güllen. Wir riechen's, wir riechen's an der Luft, an der Güllener Luft' (*Act 1*). They are speaking like children, while at the same time reinforcing the ironic play on words that is the name of the town of 'Güllen'; by chanting that they have arrived in Güllen and that they can smell it in the air, they stress the rottenness of this place.

A further form of incantation which underlines the collective nature of the chorus occurs when they share one sentence and speak as one.

> **Key quotation**
>
> DER ERSTE Ist aber Kläri.
>
> DER ZWEITE Kläri Wäscher.
>
> DER DRITTE Hier aufgewachsen.
>
> DER VIERTE Ihr Vater war Baumeister.
>
> (*Act 1*)

Here, Dürrenmatt's choice of sentence structure ('Satzbau') reveals facts about Klara's past in a staccato way using simple phrases. Four people sharing the one sentence points to the fact that all of the chorus saw her grow up, that all of the chorus have a link with her and that they are all implicated in her story.

Sometimes the chorus delivers individual short sentences and sometimes it delivers a single sentence, showing that the members of the chorus are bound together.

Key quotation

DER MALER Der D-Zug!

DER ERSTE Hält!

DER ZWEITE: In Güllen!

DER DRITTE Im verarmtesten –

DER VIERTE lausigsten –

DER ERSTE erbärmlichsten Nest der Strecke Venedig–Stockholm!
(Act 1)

The style of delivery leaves the audience in no doubt about the dilapidated state of the town and that all the citizens are upset about this. The plaintive overtones of the shared sentence stress how susceptible they would be to any promise of improvement.

Aufgabe 3

Wenn Sie eine sprachliche Analyse des Theaterstücks machen, können Sie die folgenden Erläuterungen benutzen. Welche Erläuterung passt zu welchem Titel?

a. Gesagtes wird echoartig wiederholt.

b. Gefühle, die auf spätere Handlungen hinweisen

c. Kurze Äußerungen mehrerer Personen werden zu einer Aussage aneinandergereiht.

d. mechanisches Nachplappern

e. Es werden ganze Sätze in Bestandteile zerlegt und auf mehrere Sprecher verteilt.

---

singsanghafte Wiederholung   Vorahnungen   Satzdekonstruierung

Verdoppelung   kollektiver Satzbau

Symbolism ('Symbolismus')

The black panther

Symbols ('Symbole') are objects or living things which represent something else. In *Der Besuch der alten Dame*, the most powerful symbol is the black panther, which arrives with Claire at the station. The big cat symbolises strength and elegance, as well as sexual potency when interpreted in the context of Alfred Ill's youthful affair with Klara Wäscher. Klara gave Ill the pet name of 'black panther' because he was courageous and strong, whereas the big cat which accompanies her in the play is caged, symbolising Ill's entrapment in the petty, middle-aged lifestyle to which he has grown accustomed. The panther's bid for freedom fails as he is hunted down by the citizens.

> **Key quotation**
>
> DER BUTLER Der Panther ist entwichen.
>
> CLAIRE ZACHANASSIN Hat man ihn getroffen?
>
> DER BUTLER Er liegt tot vor Ills Laden.
> (*Act 2*)

The dead body of the big cat anticipates Ill's own death at the hands of the citizens. Just as the panther fails to run away, so too Ill's bid to leave the town by train fails. He is not physically restrained but succumbs to the psychological terror which the citizens have instilled in him. He stays to die. Once Claire has orchestrated the death of Ill, his status as her black panther is restored: 'Er ist wieder so, wie er war, vor langer Zeit, der schwarze Panther. Deck ihn zu' (*Act 3*).

Black panther: Claire's unusual pet and her pet name for Ill

She has captured the Alfred she loved in her youth, so his status, in death, can be elevated back to a courageous and potent creature.

As well as symbolising potency, the black panther also demonstrates that nature is powerless against the technical progress of the world. Dürrenmatt wants to emphasise that the consumerism of the 1950s has caused the decline of the natural environment. The woodland is represented by the citizens as a simulation of the place it once was. The Teacher, who announces the death of the panther, refers to the cat as a zoological rarity which threatened mankind, but which was nevertheless precious.

> **Key quotations**
>
> DER LEHRER Wir sind aus einer großen Gefahr errettet worden. Der schwarze Panther schlich unheilbrütend durch unsere Gassen. Doch wenn wir auch befreit aufatmen, so beklagen wir dennoch den Tod einer so kostbaren zoologischen Rarität. Die Tierwelt wird ärmer, wo Menschen hausen [...]
> *(Act 2)*

Yellow shoes

The yellow shoes of the townspeople are also an important symbol in the play. Ill notices the shoes during Act 2. The shoes are bought on credit ('auf Pump/Kredit') and stand for the Gülleners' new buying power. However, since they have apparently rejected Claire's offer of a billion in exchange for the death of Ill, Ill is suspicious about where the affluence is coming from. The shoes symbolise their disloyalty to Ill, as they can only be paid for with money secured through his death. When Ill sees that the Police Officer and the Mayor are also wearing the shoes, it dawns upon him that the citizens will betray him and that they are, despite their claims to the contrary, already no longer behind him: 'ILL Auch Sie' *(Act 2)*.

The use of language in this scene echoes the biblical scene from the Gospel of Matthew, in which Christ realises that one of the disciples will betray him.

When the evening came, Jesus was reclining at the table with the Twelve. And while they were eating, he said, 'Truly, I will tell you, one of you will betray me.' They were very sad and began to say to him one after the other, 'Surely you don't mean me, Lord?' Jesus replied, 'The one who has dipped his hand in the bowl with me will betray me.'
Matthew 26: 20–23 [NIV]

Yellow is often used in Christian art for the colour of the traitor Judas's robes. In Western culture the colour yellow, though associated with gold and therefore riches, also has the negative connotations of cowardice, envy, greed and decadence. These characteristics correspond to those of the townspeople. They are greedy for the legacy from Claire and, although they have no money, they allow themselves to drift into a state of decadence. The yellow shoes link them all together, complicit in their soul-selling.

> **Aufgabe 4**
>
> Stellen Sie sich vor, dass Sie während einer Theateraufführung ein Foto von den gelben Schuhen geschossen haben. Schreiben Sie dazu einen kurzen Text (maximal 80 Wörter). Erklären Sie die Bedeutung dieser gelben Schuhe.

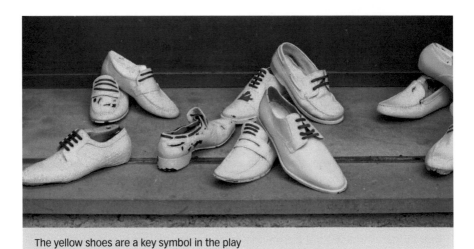

The yellow shoes are a key symbol in the play

Red and black

Although this production omitted the red underskirt, a stylised combination of black, white and red was used to reflect Dürrenmatt's symbolism

In addition to the colour symbolism of the shoes, Dürrenmatt uses the colours of red and black to illustrate the interdependency of love and death. The red hair of Claire's youth, referred to retrospectively in the play, informs the audience that she was a vibrant, vital young woman, as well as a wild and unpredictable creature. Claire is handed a red rose upon arrival in Güllen, symbolising the love that she and Ill shared in youth. As a 62-year-old woman, she still retains the red hair of her childhood, suggesting that the flame of love still burns; however, the colour is artificial and contains overtones of decadence.

Contrasting with the red of her hair and of her underskirt, of which the audience catches glimpses from time to time, is the black apparel of the old lady. The blackness of impending death is thus positioned alongside the redness of erstwhile passion and love. Claire insists that the black coffin accompanies her wherever she goes. This reminder – that the coffin will eventually be filled with a body – is a sinister symbol for Ill to contemplate.

The red underskirt is also a symbol of Claire's love for Ill in the past: 'Ich wischte dir das Blut aus dem Gesicht mit meinem roten Unterrock' (Act 3).

The bell

A third symbol may be seen in the bell. The fire bell rings when Claire approaches the station, suggesting imminent danger: 'DER PFARRER Die Feuerglocke bimmelt. Die ist noch nicht versetzt' (*Act 1*). When it rings in the first scene, the Güllen citizens are as yet unaware that this bell will signal the betrayal of Ill. The new bell which is acquired on credit by the Priest is also a symbol of the pending betrayal: 'DER PFARRER [...] Flieh, die Glocke dröhnt in Güllen, die Glocke des Verrats' (*Act 2*).

The bell sounds during the play, ringing in a new era that has begun in Güllen. It is an acoustic portent for a community which has been abandoned by God.

> **Key quotation**
>
> DER BÜRGERMEISTER [...] die Milliardärin ist unsere einzige Hoffnung.
>
> DER PFARRER Außer Gott.
>
> DER BÜRGERMEISTER Außer Gott.
>
> DER LEHRER Aber der zahlt nicht.
>
> DER MALER Der hat uns vergessen.
> (*Act 1*)

No bells ring when Ill is carried out in his coffin, symbolising the community's final severing of the link with a benign God.

> **Aufgabe 5**
>
> Stellen Sie nun weitere Recherchen zu den Symbolen an. Was stellen die folgenden Symbole dar?
>
> - das Fehlen von Uhren in Güllen
> - die symbolische Funktion von Plakaten (am Bahnhof, in Ills Laden)
> - die Zigarren, die Claire und andere Güllener rauchen

Symbolism

Objects and events in the play can hold symbolic value. When writing about symbols, you need to explain how they reveal their hidden meaning and the effect this has in the play. They may connect to a specific character: for example, the Police Officer's new gold tooth is a symbol of his abnegation of his responsibilities:

Gelb ist die Farbe des Wohlstands; der Polizist hat beispielsweise ‚einen neuen blitzenden Goldzahn'. Dieses Symbol zeigt uns einerseits, dass auch der Polizist dem Konsum von neuen Gütern und somit dem Wohlstand verfallen ist. Andererseits steht der Goldzahn auch als Symbol dafür, dass der Polizist am Komplott gegen Ill beteiligt ist.

An event may provide a metaphor indicating a future event:

Der Panther und dessen Tötung ist eine Metapher für den bevorstehenden Tod von Ill.

Satire and irony

Satire is a genre of literature which exposes vice and stupidity, often using **ironic** humour. The main object of Dürrenmatt's derision is a society which believes that money can buy everything. He does, however, satirise many other foibles of human nature and civilisation.

> **satire** *die Satire* criticising the vices or stupidity of others through humour, ridicule, exaggeration or irony
>
> **ironic** *ironisch* meaning the opposite of what you actually say

The supposedly democratic practices of local government are satirised in Act 3, when the community assembles to vote on whether Ill should die. Dürrenmatt grew up in Switzerland. One unique aspect of Switzerland's constitution is that it requires its citizens to vote on many decisions through referenda. Dürrenmatt makes an ironic comment on Swiss democracy in the farcical portrayal of a rerun of the vote, just because the press camera breaks down.

Dürrenmatt satirises the pillars of village community life: the Police Officer, the Mayor, the Priest and the Teacher. Despite the moral and civic integrity that their roles would suggest, Claire knows they will succumb to the lure of her money and thus implicate themselves in Ill's death. The satire manifests itself in four premonitions ('Vorahnungen') which Claire expresses early in the play:

- She asks the policemen whether he occasionally turns a blind eye to things.
- She asks the Priest if he comforts those who have been condemned to death.
- She suggests that the Doctor might choose 'heart attack' as the cause of death on a death certificate in future.
- When questioned by the Mayor about bringing a coffin to Güllen, she says she thinks she might need one.

The Teacher is satirised further in the speech which he delivers to the citizens before they vote on Ill's fate. His style of address and the resultant rapturous applause echo the emphatic speeches given by Adolf Hitler during National Socialist rallies.

> **Key quotation**
>
> DER LEHRER [...] Ideale, für die unsere Altvordern gelebt und gestritten hatten und für die sie gestorben sind, die den Wert unseres Abendlandes ausmachen! *Riesenbeifall.* Die Freiheit steht auf dem Spiel, wenn die Nächstenliebe verletzt, das Gebot, die Schwachen zu schützen, mißachtet, die Ehe beleidigt, ein Gericht getäuscht, eine junge Mutter ins Elend gestoßen wird. *Pfuirufe.*
> *(Act 3)*

Aufgabe 6

Erklären Sie schriftlich die Satire in diesen beiden Zitaten.

a.

> DER DRITTE Dabei waren wir eine Kulturstadt.
> DER ZWEITE Eine der ersten im Lande.
> DER ERSTE In Europa.
> DER VIERTE Goethe hat hier übernachtet. [...]
> DER DRITTE Brahms ein Quartett komponiert.
> *(Act 1)*

b.

> DER PFÄNDUNGSBEAMTE Herr Bürgermeister vergessen das Güllener Heimatmuseum.
>
> DER BÜRGERMEISTER Schon vor drei Jahren nach Amerika verkauft. Unsere Kassen sind leer. Kein Mensch bezahlt Steuern.
> *(Act 1)*

An integral part of Dürrenmatt's satire is his use of irony. With irony, what is said is not what is meant. In Act 1, Claire explains to the Mayor that she would like to give the town a billion, in return for justice. The Mayor replies, 'Die Gerechtigkeit kann man doch nicht kaufen' *(Act 1)*. This turns out to be precisely the topic of the Teacher's rallying speech near the end of the play, when the excuse of defending justice for Claire is a euphemism for defending the citizens' desire for wealth. So, Claire does buy her justice and she always knew that she would be able to do it. She just needed to wait.

In Act 2, the contradictions between what the townspeople say and do are ironic. With the example of extreme wealth suspended above Ill's shop, in the form of Claire on her balcony, the townspeople say that money cannot buy everything. They then immediately buy on credit.

> **Key quotation**
>
> DER ZWEITE Für Geld kann man eben alles haben. *Er spuckt aus.*
>
> DER ERSTE Nicht bei uns. *Er schlägt mit der Faust auf den Tisch.*
>
> ILL Dreiundzwanzig achtzig.
>
> DER ZWEITE Schreib's auf.
>
> *(Act 2)*

Another example of irony is the Police Officer's suggestion that they investigate whether Claire is indeed inciting the townspeople to murder, in a sober ('nüchtern') manner, while he is drinking beer.

> **Key quotation**
>
> DER POLIZIST Merkwürdig. Äußerst merkwürdig. *Er trinkt Bier.*
>
> ILL Die natürlichste Sache der Welt.
>
> DER POLIZIST Lieber Ill, so natürlich ist die Sache nicht. Untersuchen wir den Fall nüchtern.
>
> *(Act 2)*

At the start of Act 2 the citizens are seemingly supporting Ill, referring to his becoming Mayor in the spring. However, they reinforce their remark with the word 'todsicher' ('dead certain'), ironically predicting his death.

Ironic allusions ('ironische Anspielungen') are also made on several occasions to figures from history, drama and opera. Each allusion suggests, with black humour, what may be in store for the characters later in the play, or else what Dürrenmatt thinks of the characters.

Aufgabe 7

Lesen Sie die untenstehenden Anspielungen, die im Theaterstück vorkommen. Recherchieren Sie, was sie bedeuten und erklären Sie, warum Dürrenmatt sie benutzt:

a. Die Enkelkinder vom Bürgermeister heißen Hermine und Adolfine (*Akt 1, Seite 29*).

b. Der Lehrer vergleicht Ill und Claire mit Romeo und Julia (*Akt 1, Seite 35*).

c. Im Radio spielt Musik aus der Oper *Die Lustige Witwe* (*Akt 2, Seite 64*).

There are also examples of paradox ('die Paradoxie') in the drama. In Act 1, all trains are on time despite none of the townpeople having a watch. Another paradox is the name of the Mayor's wife: Annette Dummermuth ('dumm' meaning 'stupid'), who was the best pupil in the class.

Writing about language

Examining the kind of language used in a play such as *Der Besuch der alten Dame* is always a useful way to understand the playwright's attitude to his subject matter.

In preparing to write about language, you might want to memorise a few examples of sentences which illustrate irony, symbolism or Dürrenmatt's character-specific language choices. Always ask yourself: how does Dürrenmatt's choice of language affect an understanding of the scene, character or play?

Useful phrases

Bei der Analyse der Sprache, die im Theaterstück verwendet wird, ... When analysing the language used in the play, ...

die Sprache, die Claire verwendet the language that is used by Claire

aus der Sicht des Schriftstellers/Zuschauers from the point of view of the playwright/audience

Wenn man ... beachtet/untersucht ... When one considers/examines ...

Im Laufe der Tragikomödie wird es immer offensichtlicher, dass ... In the course of the tragicomedy, it becomes more and more evident that ...

Wir sehen sofort ... We immediately see ...

Wir werden mit ... konfrontiert. We are faced with ...

Ein wichtiger Bezugspunkt ist ... An important point of reference is ...

Der Höhepunkt kommt, wenn ... The climax comes when ...

... thematisieren to take ... as a central theme

Es lässt an (+ acc) ... denken. It suggests/evokes ...

Ein Symbolort für Claires und Ills frühere Liebe ist der Konradsweilerwald. A symbolic place for Claire and Ill's early love is the Konradsweiler wood.

Die Farbe Schwarz/Rot steht für ... The colour black/red stands for ...

Die/Der ... spielt ebenfalls eine bedeutsame Rolle, denn ... The ... also plays a significant role because ...

Gelb kommt aber nicht nur im Zusammenhang mit den Schuhen vor, sondern auch ... Yellow crops up, not just in connection with the shoes but also ...

Vocabulary

die **Analyse** analysis
analysieren to analyse
aufrichtig frank, sincere
der **Chor** chorus
der **Dialog** dialogue
die **Direktheit** directness
der **Effekt** effect
die **Erzählung** narrative
die **Erzählperspektive** point of view (literary term)
einen Gegensatz bilden to form a contrast
die **Handlung** the plot
die **Perspektive** perspective

der **Satzbau** sentence structure
die **Sichtweise** point of view
die **Sprache** language
untersuchen to analyse
unverblümt blunt
das **Vokabular** vocabulary
die **Vorgeschichte** backstory, prologue
wirken to have an effect
die **Wirkung** effect
eine Wirkung haben to have an effect
der **Wortschatz** vocabulary
die **Wortstellung** word order
zweideutig ambiguous

Friedrich Dürrenmatt was a keen observer of human behaviour within 20th-century society, which led him to explore several themes in *Der Besuch der alten Dame:* the rise of consumerism and the corresponding decline in moral values; love and death; the interchangeability of justice and revenge; and the vulnerability of impoverished communities to the rise of dictators or saviour figures. As you read the play, you should note where the playwright seeks to communicate these themes.

The rise of consumerism and decline in moral values

At the beginning of Act 1, the audience is introduced to a town where economic confidence and material wealth are now unknown. The citizens have witnessed their industry decline and their living conditions deteriorate, in marked contrast to the success that neighbouring communities have enjoyed. Dürrenmatt portrays a group of people ripe for rescue. He had witnessed small towns in Switzerland lose their autonomy in the post-war years and his play mirrors some of the concerns that he felt about the loss of community identity.

Before Claire Zachanassian announces the nature of the 'deal' that will reverse the town's fortunes, the citizens of Güllen are depicted as a group of mutually-supportive people who are prepared to wheedle and inveigle to secure material benefits for the collective good.

> **Key quotation**
>
> ILL [...] Die Zachanassian soll mit ihren Millionen herausrücken.
>
> DER BÜRGERMEISTER Millionen – das ist genau die richtige Auffassung. (*Act 1*)

When they are made aware of the 'deal', their collective reaction is one of moral abhorrence. The Mayor explains that Western values are synonymous with human values, so the suggestion of exchanging a billion for a human life is out of the question: 'Frau Zachanassian: Noch sind wir in Europa, noch sind wir keine Heiden. Ich lehne im Namen der Stadt Güllen das Angebot ab' (*Act 1*). Claire and Dürrenmatt know, however, that the offer will continue to plague the minds of the citizens, who have been deprived of material comforts for years. Claire's ironic observation, 'Ich warte' (*Act 1*) is a premonition of the citizens' inevitable yielding to temptation.

In Act 2, the townspeople taste the delights of spending money on credit and are shown to be too ignorant or self-deluded to recognise that their yellow shoes unite them in the betrayal of Ill. The parliamentary and political institutions fail him, as do the justice system, the press and the Church. So, too, does the education system, represented by the Teacher, who quotes the Classics of Literature. Initially uneasy with the materialistic desires of the other citizens, he finally concedes that society is powerless to resist the lure of money and that Ill's fate will be the fate of many more people to come if they attempt to do so.

> **Key quotation**
>
> DER LEHRER […] Man wird Sie töten. Ich weiß es […] Die Versuchung ist zu groß und unsere Armut zu bitter. […] Ich fühle, wie ich langsam zu einem Mörder werde. […] Ich fürchte mich, Ill, so wie Sie sich gefürchtet haben.
> (*Act 3*)

In contrast to the moral decline and fall of the citizens through the lure of money, Ill develops from a self-deluded liar and opportunist into a courageous man who confronts his responsibilities. By Act 3, he is still dressed in shabby clothes which act as a foil to the fine garb of the citizens. The poor man embodying moral fortitude represents the triumph of human decency over capitalist principles. The chorus, by contrast, finishes the play with an ode to the terrors of poverty and the joys of having money.

> **Key quotation**
>
> CHOR I Ungeheuer ist viel
>
>   Gewaltige Erdbeben
>
>   Feuerspeiende Berge, Fluten des Meeres […]
>
> CHOR II Doch nichts ist ungeheurer als die Armut
> (*Act 3*)

As discussed on pages 45–46, this chorus is a parody of the final chorus from the Greek tragedy, *Antigone*. While the Greek chorus speaks of the subjugation of nature by man, the chorus in *Der Besuch der alten Dame* turns things on their head. They sing of the fear of natural catastrophes but conclude that no natural disaster, be it earthquake or atomic bomb, can be as fearsome as being poor. The Greek chorus was included in tragedies to help the audience understand important, fundamental truths, but Dürrenmatt's chorus celebrates the triumph of its own supreme selfishness.

> **Aufgabe 1**
>
> ‚Geld regiert die Welt.'
>
> Nennen Sie fünf symbolische Gegenstände im Schauspiel, die diese Hypothese unterstützen. Wie effektiv tun sie dies?

Tips for assessment

You need to be able to write about the presentation of themes in relation to other elements of the play, such as their effect on characters, or how they drive and influence the direction of the plot.

For example, when discussing the theme of consumerism you might observe:

> Der Mensch ist zu schwach, den Verlockungen des Konsums zu widerstehen.

Then link to how Dürrenmatt shows weakness through the character of the Priest:

> Sogar der Pfarrer, ein Diener Gottes, erliegt der Versuchung des Kaufwahns, als er eine neue Kirchenglocke auf Kredit kauft. Dem Priester scheint allerdings klar zu sein, dass dies eine Schwäche ist, wenn er zu Ill sagt: ,Flieh! Wir sind schwach'.

Love and death

The distortion of love in Western society

Dürrenmatt wanted to show that a society which respects material goods excessively is the direct opposite of a society which extends love and tenderness towards others. During several nostalgic reminiscences between Claire and Ill in the Konradsweiler woodland, the audience is given to understand that they shared a loving relationship when they were young. The happiness of this love coloured their impressions of the environment where they met, so the audience hears descriptions of beautiful sounds and sights of nature.

> **Key quotation**
>
> ILL Es ist wie einst, wie wir jung waren und kühn, da wir in den Konradsweilerwald gingen, in den Tagen unserer Liebe. Die Sonne hoch über den Tannen, eine helle Scheibe. Ferne Wolkenzüge und das Rufen des Kuckucks irgendwo in der Wurzelwildernis.
> (Act 1)

Dürrenmatt exposes romantic love as weak in the face of market forces. The young love of Klara and Ill was sacrificed for material gain, as Ill succeeded in escaping his financial obligations to be a father to Klara's child and married Mathilde because her family owned a shop. During the play, the audience is given to understand that the marriage has not been a romantic one. Ill chose to forego love and Klara, too, was obliged to forget love and settle for a life of prostitution in which love was a commodity.

Claire's capacity for marrying and discarding her husbands – apart from Zachanassian himself, who rescued her from her days in the brothel – appears to be a humiliating and debasing process for the men, but equates with the degradation that she experienced when she was forced to satisfy men's sexual appetites in the brothel. Love does not feature in the comical string of marriages she has made and Dürrenmatt seems to be suggesting that marriage is an empty institution.

The disintegration of youthful love into something quite abhorrent can be seen in Dürrenmatt's decision to represent the 62-year-old Claire as a conglomeration of prosthetic parts. Romantic love is grotesquely parodied when Ill seeks to kiss Claire's hand in Act 1 and discovers that the hand is cold and made of ivory. The comic allusions to Claire's needing to reassemble her body from time to time underline that any possibility of rekindling physical passion between Ill and Claire is remote. By the beginning of Act 3, when Claire is seen dressed as a bride in the Petersche barn, macabre elements are in place for her imminent claim on Ill's life. The Priest's choice of Bible reading at Claire's latest wedding, a verse extolling the importance of love, serves to underline the travesty of love that her feelings towards Ill have, in reality, become.

 And now these three remain: faith, hope and love. But the greatest of these is love.
1 Corinthians 13:13 [NIV]

For Claire, the only way to retrieve past love is to immortalise it in the mausoleum on Capri. The price of preserving their love will be Ill's death. Dressed in white, she is reunited with the man whom she remembers as her black panther: **'Er ist wieder so, wie er war, vor langer Zeit, der schwarze Panther. Deck ihn zu'** (*Act 3*).

Just as passionate love is shown to be past, so, too, family love is notably absent in the play, apart from fawning and sentimental comments made by Ill about his children. By the beginning of Act 2, even before Claire's offer has started to affect the town's attitude to him, his son, daughter and wife are keen to avoid their father's company: he wants them to join him for breakfast and they find excuses not to do so.

In Act 3, the family members have become so obsessed by their fur coats, low-cut dresses and sports car, that they have no time to support Ill as a husband and father before the council hearing. They drive off to watch a film instead. Love is significantly absent in their parting cries.

Key quotation

DIE TOCHTER So long, Daddy.
FRAU ILL Auf bald! Auf bald!
(*Act 3*)

The inevitability of death

Just as love happened before the play began, so too will death inevitably happen before the play ends. The price that Ill will pay for the debasement of his and Klara's romantic love will be his own death, and Dürrenmatt hints at this inexorable fate throughout the play.

The arrival of the coffin with its retinue of eccentric 'mourners' and its floral 'tributes' is a clear **harbinger** of death.

Various plays on words ('Wortspiele') allude to death too, such as Ill's reference to Claire's golden sense of humour when she asks the acrobat if he has ever strangled someone: 'Einen goldenen Humor besitzt die Klara! Zum Totlachen, diese Bonmots' (*Act 1*). While Ill wishes to be complimentary with this reference, the association of 'golden' with 'yellow' actually hints at rottenness too and alludes to Ill's destiny.

Claire's initial encounters with the Doctor, the Mayor and the Priest all contain overtones of death: she asks the Doctor if he is accustomed to writing death certificates; she tells the Mayor that she will perhaps make use of the coffin soon; and she suggests to the Priest that the death penalty could be brought back.

When Claire announces her 'deal' at the end of Act 1, the stage directions demand a deathly silence from the townspeople. The tolling of the bell evokes a funereal tone, particularly in the scene when Ill attempts to flee the town via the station. Reference is made here briefly to the **Passion Plays** of Oberammergau, suggesting that a human sacrifice similar to that of Christ is imminent.

Ill tries to leave the town but fails; it is then that he realises the inevitability of his death

harbinger *der Vorbote* a herald or forewarning

Passion Plays *die Passionsspiele* plays performed at Easter depicting the trial, suffering and death of Jesus Christ

By Act 3, the town artist is painting the figure of Christ, which takes the audience one stage further along the path to death.

Two vividly physical images which represent death can be seen in the plethora of guns carried by the citizens in Act 2 to 'protect' themselves from the escaped panther, and in the axe which is for sale in Ill's shop in Act 3 and to which the press refer as being a murder tool.

An auditory reminder of death occurs in Act 2, when Roby is asked by Claire to play a funeral march on his guitar. The choir, under the leadership of the Teacher, then takes up the tune, frightening Ill, who is aware of his impending doom: 'ILL Auf meinen Tod übt ihr dieses Lied, auf meinen Tod' (*Act 2*).

In the appendix to the play, Dürrenmatt considers whether Ill's death is meaningful or senseless. Such a death, accepted by way of atonement for his sins, would have been a noble and justified death in ancient tragedy and, therefore, it could be seen as meaningful for Ill as an individual. However, as a death set in a contemporary town such as Güllen, where so little makes sense, it seems that Ill dies a senseless death. Dürrenmatt's comedies are an attempt to regard the world from a critical distance.

> **Key quotation**
>
> [Ill] wird groß durch sein Sterben (sein Tod ermangle nicht einer gewissen Monumentalität). Sein Tod ist sinnvoll und sinnlos zugleich. Sinnvoll allein wäre er im mythischen Reich einer antiken Polis, nun spielt sich die Geschichte in Güllen ab. In der Gegenwart.
> *(Anhang, Anmerkung 1)*

Aufgabe 2

a. Übersetzen Sie den folgenden Text, der das Liebesmotiv mit dem Todesmotiv vergleicht, ins Englische:

> In dieser Tragikomödie wird die Liebe mehrmals durch die Farbe Rot repräsentiert. Zum Beispiel bekommt Claire schon bei der Ankunft ‚rote Rosen' in die Hand gedrückt. Dass Liebe sehr nah in Verbindung mit Tod steht, ist auch klar, denn Claire hat schon bei der Ankunft einen schwarzen Sarg dabei, der auf Ills späteren Tod vorausweist.

b. Geben Sie ein weiteres Beispiel aus dem Theaterstück, in dem Liebe und Tod einander gegenübergestellt werden.

Justice or revenge?

The play introduces the theme of justice early on, when Ill refers to Klara's keen sense of fair play when she was a young girl. He alludes to it with respect and the Mayor immediately wishes to include this quality of Klara's character in his welcome speech: 'Klara liebte die Gerechtigkeit. Ausgeprochen' (*Act 1*).

The emphasis on her extreme love for justice foreshadows the monstrous turn that this will take later in the play. Once the terms of her offer have been made clear to the town, Claire reiterates her desire for recompense: '[...] und nun will ich Gerechtigkeit, Gerechtigkeit für eine Milliarde' (*Act 1*).

The restyling of a search for justice into a desire for personal revenge becomes apparent by the end of Act 1. Claire makes it plain that she is buying justice because she can afford to do so: 'Ich kann sie mir leisten' (*Act 1*).

The weakness of the legal system

The injustice wrought upon Klara by the court when she applied for support for her pregnancy has precipitated her lifelong pursuit of a vendetta against Alfred Ill. Dürrenmatt was critical of the petty narrow-mindedness of Swiss local government in the 1950s and shows his audience twice in the play how inefficient and farcical their procedures can be. Perjured evidence was accepted in the courtroom the first time and, in the second hearing, when the citizens assemble to decide Ill's fate, the need to vote twice is accepted because the press lighting system fails. These examples of judicial failings invite the audience to consider whether an individual really has the right to adopt a 'vigilante' stance to seek personal retribution.

The corruption of the legal system

The susceptibility of the judiciary to corruption is shown further in the Priest's early reference to capital punishment being illegal in Switzerland: 'Die Todesstrafe ist in unserem Land abgeschafft, gnädige Frau' (*Act 1*). After the vote to end Ill's life, this law of the land has been pushed conveniently aside so that the citizens can accept the Claire Zachanassian Foundation in the name of justice, not money. Claire has been able to override the judicial system and impose her own rule of law on several occasions. She bought the lives of Toby and Roby, who had been sentenced to death in America, thus proving the disreputable state of the American judiciary. The figures of the Police Officer and the Mayor – pillars of society – are shown as fallible men who can turn from obsequious flatterers into duplicitous traitors and, ultimately, aggressive henchmen: 'DER POLIZIST Steh auf, du Schwein. *Er reißt ihn in die Höhe*' (*Act 3*).

> **Aufgabe 3**
>
> **a.** Lesen Sie den folgenden Artikel aus dem SWR2-Programm, der sich mit dem Begriff ‚Gerechtigkeit' im Theaterstück *Der Besuch der alten Dame* befasst. Fassen Sie den Inhalt in Ihren eigenen Worten zusammen (ungefähr 80 Wörter).

Mit dem Konflikt ‚Geld oder Moral' – dem zentralen Thema des Stückes – hat Dürrenmatt ins Schwarze ewiger menschlicher Widersprüche getroffen*. Der Begriff von Gerechtigkeit, den Dürrenmatt hier ins Spiel bringt, beginnt sofort vieldeutig und widersprüchlich zu schillern**. Kann Gerechtigkeit tatsächlich käuflich sein?

Obwohl die Güllener sich zunächst weigern, ihren Mitbürger Alfred Ill umzubringen, bekommt Claire schließlich ihren Willen. Dieses moralische Einknicken*** vor den Verlockungen des Geldes wurde lange als Versagen interpretiert, als typisch bürgerliche Doppelmoral, als Korrumpierbarkeit, Opportunismus, Mitläufertum†.

Gemeinwohl vs. Moral

Sieht man allerdings genauer hin, dann erscheint es etwas zu einfach, das Verhalten der Güllener Bürger allein auf Gier und Herdentrieb‡ zurückzuführen. Schließlich geht es in dem Stück um die erheblich komplexere Frage, wie in einer Krisensituation zu entscheiden wäre, wenn auf der einen Seite das Gemeinwohl und auf der anderen die Moral auf dem Spiel steht.

* **ins Schwarze treffen** to hit the mark   ** **schillern** to glitter

*** **das Einknicken** caving in   † **das Mitläufertum** followership

‡ **der Herdentrieb** herd instinct

b. Was ist Ihre Meinung: Steht das Gemeinwohl über der Moral? Verfassen Sie einen Blog, in dem Sie Ihre Ideen erläutern.

Aufgabe 4

a. Friedrich Dürrenmatt war der Meinung, dass Gerechtigkeit und Freiheit innerhalb der Gesellschaft nicht nebeneinander existieren können. Inwiefern hat er recht? Verfassen Sie eine schriftliche Stellungnahme von nicht mehr als 100 Wörtern.

b. Wie verstehen Claire, Ill und die Güllener das Thema Gerechtigkeit?

Tips for assessment

In your exam you may wish to quote critical opinions you have read. Although you might not agree with every critical view you read, an alternative perspective could come in handy as a counterargument to your own point of view. Always make sure you acknowledge any critical opinion you include.

Saviour or dictator?

As discussed earlier, the contextual backdrop to *Der Besuch der alten Dame* spans both world wars and the periods of economic decline and growth around them in Europe, particularly within Germany. During the period of financial depression in the 1920s and 1930s, Adolf Hitler and his National Socialist Party came to prominence. Der Besuch der alten Dame is not an allegory for Germany's transformation into the Nazi **Third Reich**, but it is possible to draw several thematic comparisons between how Germany came to follow Adolf Hitler and how the citizens of Güllen come to follow Claire.

From glory to disgrace

During the late 19th century, Germany was a strong country. However, after the First World War the country struggled to recover. The German people needed a way out of their hardship and this contributed to the perception of Adolf Hitler as a saviour, offering a collective identity, economic revival and hope for a better future. This theme of a saviour is mirrored in the play. The people of Güllen had clearly enjoyed cultural glory and industrial success in the past, when Ill and Claire were young, but for an unaccountable reason – we only learn later that the ruin of Güllen was a deliberate ploy by Claire – they have fallen on hard times. When Claire arrives, her wealth and its possibilities for the town are eagerly discussed; she is treated with reverence.

Claire's ambiguity as a saviour or dictator is suggested in the way she and others describe her. She is referred to as a witch-like creature ('Zauberhexchen' (*Act 1*); 'eine verteufelt schöne Hexe' (*Act 1*)) and she describes herself as hellish too: '[…] ich bin die Hölle geworden' (*Act 1*). To some extent, Claire can be equated with evil, just as Hitler became the personification of evil. Hitler felt that he was treated unfairly by Jewish professors at the School of Arts at the University of Vienna, where his application to become a student was rejected, just as Claire's paternity suit against Ill was rejected. Claire's patience allows the greed – or desperation – of the townspeople to grow. As she 'waits', the collective spirit in Güllen gains momentum in Act 2, when the depressed and deprived citizens realise that Claire's offer will make them as rich as their neighbouring towns. They just need to justify their change of loyalty by claiming to act in the cause of justice.

Unlike the German people, who maintained that they had been unaware of **the Holocaust**, the townspeople consciously move from a stance of abhorrence at the thought of Ill being murdered, to justifying his death on the basis that it will herald the start of a new time of prosperity for them.

Third Reich *das Dritte Reich* the period of German history when Adolf Hitler was in power, 1933–1945

the Holocaust *der Holocaust* the period of persecution and extermination of European Jews by Nazi Germany

A woman, not a man

Dürrenmatt's choice of a maligned woman as the focus of dictatorial power is unusual. In the 1950s when the play was first performed, the role of women in Swiss society was insecure and insignificant and, although Dürrenmatt does not actually set his play specifically in Switzerland (rather, just 'somewhere in Europe'), he was very conscious that he was portraying a male-dominated community. The playwright alludes to the diminished role of women in the council meeting in Act 3, when all women, including Claire, are told to await the outcome in an anteroom. However, in Claire's plain-speaking, unemotional **rhetoric** and clever diction, he demonstrates a certain contempt for men: *'Ich saß als Kind stundenlang auf dem Dach und spuckte hinunter. Aber nur auf die Männer'* (*Act 1*).

Claire is a woman but not womanly, as her prosthetic body emphasises. Her power is both mystical – she says that she cannot be killed – but also infused with masculinity. She smokes cigars and spits like a man. She is androgynous.

Aufgabe 5

Inwiefern ist die Verletzbarkeit der Güllener für Ills Mord verantwortlich und inwiefern ist der Einfluss von Claire Zachanassian dafür verantwortlich? Schreiben Sie in Stichworten Ihre Gedanken zu dieser Frage auf.

---

rhetoric *die Rhetorik* language designed to have a persuasive or impressive effect

Godlessness

The Christian faith of Güllen collapses under the pressure of temptation from Claire's offer. The Catholic Church is personified in the character of the Priest, and throughout the play there are repeated allusions to God. The hotel, where Claire sits in judgement on the town of Güllen from her bedroom balcony, is called the 'Hotel of the Golden Apostle'. The name conjures images of the economic boom which is imminent (in the colour gold) but, more importantly, also suggests a place where the disciples of Christ may have gathered to preach messages of atonement. This is an ironic allusion to the role of the disciples, who do not support but, rather, betray. The building becomes the focal point for the gathering of Judas-like traitors as the play progresses, with Claire presiding here like the angry, wrathful God of the Old Testament.

By the time Ill decides to flee the town, he arrives at the station to find that it, too, has been cosmetically enhanced by anticipated wealth and is advertising trips to the Oberammergau Passion Play. The notion of the citizens taking a trip to see this production, having enacted their own crucifixion of a fellow citizen, is deeply ironic.

In addition to these allusions, Dürrenmatt makes reference to the section in the gospel of Matthew which celebrates the supremacy of love over hope and charity. The love for material wealth is the only love that is tangible by the end of the play.

The Priest urges Ill not to lead the citizens into temptation by staying in the town: 'Flieh, führe uns nicht in Versuchung, indem du bleibst' (*Act 2*). The citizens have, however, already been led into temptation by the time he utters this warning. They have been tempted not only to consider breaking the biblical commandment, 'You shall not murder' ('Du sollst nicht töten'), but also to break the first commandment, 'You shall have no other gods before me' ('Du sollst keine anderen Götter neben mir haben'), by worshipping false Gods, namely gold [NIV]. From the outset of the play, the audience is informed that Güllen is a town that has been forgotten by God.

God is only referred to in negative contexts. The 'happy ending' of consumer paradise can be interpreted as a hell on earth. Ill inverts the Priest's promise that he will pray for Ill into a warning that the Priest should pray for the souls of Güllen.

Dürrenmatt was brought up in a Christian household and from childhood onwards he loved painting the more vivid scenes he knew from the Bible, such as the battles and the Great Flood. As a young student he rebelled against his father, a pastor, and thereafter expressed an ambivalent attitude to God and the Church.

The priest begs Ill to leave and save the town from temptation

The play is not explicitly seeking to criticise the Church, but to criticise the complacency of Christian values. Dürrenmatt criticises religious institutions which purport to uphold moral goodness but which, hypocritically, behave otherwise.

Aufgabe 6

a. Finden Sie das Gespräch zwischen Ill und dem Pfarrer im zweiten Akt und übersetzen Sie die folgende Textstelle ins Englische:

Akt 2, Seite 74: *ILL Die Leute sich fröhlich. [...] DER PFARRER [...] erhalten Waffen, dies zu vermögen.*

b. Im ersten Akt sagt Claire, ,ich bin die Hölle'. Inwiefern stimmen Sie zu, dass Claire diese Hölle für Ill verursacht hat oder stimmen Sie dem Pfarrer zu, dass Ill seine eigene Hölle geschaffen hat?

c. Inwiefern stellt der Rat des Pfarrers einen Wendepunkt dar?

Guilt, trespassers and debt

Ill recognises by Act 3 that he must accept his guilt ('Schuld') in having caused Claire to suffer as a girl. The acceptance of this responsibility and recognition that only he can make amends for the wrong, by surrendering his life, leads to atonement. He becomes a tragic hero through this atonement.

All of the citizens of Güllen become trespassers or 'evil-doers' ('Schuldiger') (in the Biblical sense of the word) against Ill because they learn that they will personally inherit one half of Claire's billion, provided that they carry out Claire's wish. The lure of potential wealth causes them to start incurring debts which can only be paid for once the half-billion is earned. Through a mixture of self-delusion and collective greed, they gradually position themselves to take the life of their fellow citizen. The Priest pleads with Ill to flee the town and remove the temptation (himself) from the citizens. As the Teacher observes, however, the temptation is too strong and their poverty has made them entirely susceptible to it.

Key quotation

DER LEHRER [...] Man wird Sie töten. Ich weiß es, von Anfang an, und auch Sie wissen es schon lange, auch wenn es in Güllen sonst niemand wahrhaben will. Die Versuchung ist zu groß und unsere Armut zu bitter. (*Act 3*)

Aufgabe 7

Welche Rolle spielt Schuld in *Der Besuch der alten Dame*?

Aufgabe 8

Lesen Sie die folgenden Aussagen über die Gemeindeversammlung im dritten Akt. Welche sind richtig (R), welche falsch (F)? Korrigieren Sie die falschen Aussagen.

a. Am Anfang der Gemeindeversammlung versucht der Lehrer, alle Schuld auf Ill zu schieben.

b. Der Lehrer fordert die Güllener auf, nur dann für das Angebot zu stimmen, wenn sie in Zukunft nur mehr in Gerechtigkeit leben wollen.

c. Bei der Abstimmung stimmen alle anwesenden Personen dem Antrag des Bürgermeisters zu.

d. Ill nimmt die Entscheidung seiner Mitbürger schweigend an.

Writing about themes

Once you have identified which theme you are being asked to write about, you will need to demonstrate how that theme is presented and to be selective. As you plan, make sure you have considered all the different areas of the novel that a theme can affect: plot, structure, characters and language. Consider too, how the context of the novel has helped frame the theme within the story.

Once you have made notes on each area, you can refine them to focus your explanation of the theme and its importance. Well-chosen quotations will help support the accuracy of your assertions.

Useful phrases

Das Thema wird anhand von ... erläutert   The theme is exemplified by ...

Dieses Thema wird durch ... (weiter) entwickelt.   This theme is developed by ...

Das Thema ... wird durch die Taten von ... verstärkt.   The theme of ... is reinforced by the actions of ...

Was mich betrifft, ist das Hauptthema ...   As far as I am concerned the main theme is ...

Der Dramatiker verfolgt das Ziel, ...   The playwright is aiming at ...

Der Dramatiker enthüllt die romantische Liebe als ...   The playwright exposes romantic love as ...

An dieser viel diskutierten Frage scheiden sich die Geister.   Opinions are divided on this vexed question.

ein nicht zu unterschätzender Aspekt im Stück   an aspect in the play that should not be underestimated

... wird oft von anderen Themen in den Hintergrund gedrängt.   ... is often pushed into the background by other themes/topics.

Wir müssen uns mit der Frage auseinandersetzen, was ...   We must tackle the question of what ...

... präsentiert/<u>stellt</u> die Wirkung des Konsums auf die Charaktere <u>dar</u>.   ... presents/portrays the effect of consumerism on the characters.

Das Thema, dem ich mich jetzt widmen will, ist ...   The theme I should like to deal with now is ...

Was das Thema ... betrifft, ...   As far as the theme ... is concerned ...

Es deutet alles darauf hin, dass ...   Everything points to the fact that ...

Mehrere Hinweise deuten auf den christlichen Glauben hin.   Several allusions point to the Christian faith.

Vocabulary

andeuten to imply

deuten auf (+acc) to indicate

das Hauptthema main topic

darauf hindeuten to imply

hinweisen auf to suggest

interpretieren to interpret

einer Sache schuldig sein to be guilty of something

seine Schuld bekennen to admit one's guilt

seine Schuld sühnen to atone for ones guilt

thematisieren to address

verkörpern to embody

eine Vielfalt an/von Themen a variety of topics

die Wirklichkeit darstellen to portray reality

zeigen to indicate

die Zeile beschreibt the line describes

Before you start

The following pages are designed to give you some ideas of how you could respond to exam questions. Each exam board sets questions differently so you should make sure that you are familiar with the approach your own exam board takes. However, every question that you encounter is likely to require you to offer your interpretation of, and justifications for, the views you hold on a certain point, while making specific reference to the text.

Tips for assessment

✓ Know what format the exam questions are likely to take. For example, will questions include prompts? How many questions will you have to choose from? How many will you need to answer?

✓ Familiarise yourself with past papers.

✓ Know what will get you high marks. Have a good look at the mark scheme and examine how marks are awarded.

✓ Read the examiners' reports from previous years where available, as they will give you an insight into what the examiners will focus on.

Responding to the question

Always read the questions very carefully, so that you are sure that you are writing within the remit of what is asked. When exam boards publish their reports on how individual exam papers were completed, they always comment on students who misread questions. Read the essay question options closely and decide which suits your knowledge of the play best. Once you have chosen the question, it is good practice to underline key words in it first and it is also important that, if the question has several parts, you prepare from the outset to respond to all parts. For example:

Wie und mit welchem Erfolg benutzt Friedrich Dürrenmatt Symbole in *Der Besuch der alten Dame*?

The question is asking you *how* the playwright uses symbols, so you should make a list of instances in the play where symbolism occurs, noting simultaneously *how* the symbol is used.

The question also asks you to comment on *how successful* you think the symbolism is, so you should consider the impact of each symbol you mention. The structure of your essay might take the form of a series of paragraphs, each one of which refers to an example of a symbol and a consideration of how effective you think it is, with justification and exemplification (i.e. quotations or references to the text).

Here are some common types of question starters that might come up:

Untersuchen Sie … (*Examine …*), **Erklären Sie …** (*Explain …*) and **Kommentieren Sie …** (*Comment …*) questions require you to explore a topic in detail, using contextual knowledge where appropriate and evidence to support your view.

Analysieren Sie … (*Analyse …*) and **Beurteilen Sie …** (*Assess …*) questions require all this too but also something more: the application of your own interpretation, a deeper understanding and consideration of the topic.

Vergleichen Sie … or **Stellen Sie einen Vergleich zwischen … an** (*Compare …*) questions expect you to provide a balanced discussion of two parts, giving roughly the same amount of consideration to each before arriving at a conclusion.

Wählen Sie … (*Choose …*) questions expect a definite conclusion to be arrived at, after a thoughtful and analytical discussion.

The following **W-questions** ask you to think about more than one viewpoint or element and to assess their effect or impact:

Wie effektiv ist …?	(*How effective is…?*)
Was erfahren wir über …?	(*What do we learn about…?*)
Welche Rolle spielt/spielen …?	(*Which role does/do … play?*)
Welche Methoden benutzt der Autor …?	(*Which methods does the author use …?*)
Wie verändert sich …?	(*How does … change?*)
Wie könnte man … erklären?	(*How could one explain …?*)
Welche Bedeutung hat/haben …?	(*Which meaning does/do … have?*)
Welchen Effekt hat/haben …?	(*Which effect does/do … have?*)
Wie reagieren Sie auf …?	(*How do you react to …?*)
Welches Ziel verfolgt …?	(*What is the objective/aim of …?*)

Further important phrases that are regularly used in exam questions:

Inwiefern/Inwieweit …	(*To what extent …*)
Begründen Sie …	(*Justify …*)
Verdeutlichen Sie …	(*Illustrate …*)

At times, the question might include a quotation from the play or a statement about the play and you will be asked to respond. In these cases, common questions are:

Inwiefern bist du auch dieser Meinung?	(*To what extent are you also of this opinion?*)
Inwiefern stimmen Sie dieser Aussage zu?	(*To what extent do you agree with this statement?*)

In these cases, you have to base the core of your argument on the specific quotation or statement. You can use quotation from other parts of the play to support your arguments, but keep the question at the heart of your essay.

Planning your response

In order to answer the question thoroughly, you will need to give a structured response. Your answer should consist of an **introduction**, the **main body** and a **conclusion**. You need to structure the main body of the essay, but first note down the content you want to include. Your exam board might give you several bullet points as a guideline. Check exactly what you can expect in your own exam. For example:

> **Untersuchen Sie die Rolle von Claire Zachanassian in dem Theaterstück *Der Besuch der alten Dame*. Sie können die folgenden Stichpunkte benutzen:**
>
> - **Claire als junges Mädchen und ihre Beziehung zu Ill**
> - **Claire als erniedrigte Prostituierte**
> - **Claire als zurückkehrende ‚alte Dame', die Gerechtigkeit verlangt**
> - **Claire als Symbol der Rache.**

It is good practice to spend a few minutes of planning time compiling a list of points that will support your essay response. Planning allows you to avoid repetition or the inclusion of irrelevant points, and helps you return repeatedly to the focus of the question. Draft your plan in German to ensure you know all the necessary vocabulary before you begin writing. It will also save you time, as you will have already begun to formulate your sentences.

You could use a planning format such as a linear plan with bullet points, a mind map or a spider diagram.

Aufgabe 9

Stellen Sie sich vor, dass Sie die folgende Prüfungsaufgabe bekommen.

> **Was sind Ihrer Meinung nach die Schwächen und Stärken von Ill *oder* Claire? (Konzentrieren Sie sich auf *eine* Person!)**

Bevor Sie diese Frage schriftlich beantworten, bereiten Sie sich vor, indem Sie die Diagramme vervollständigen. Sie können dabei auch an Charaktereigenschaften denken.

Claires Stärken	Claires Schwächen
• unabhängig	• unversöhnlich
• entschlossen und geduldig	• von Rache besessen

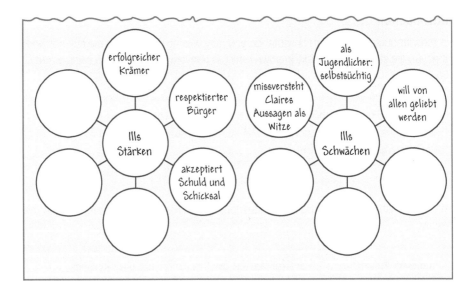

Tips for assessment

In a question like this, in which you have a choice of focus, ensure your answer focuses on Claire *or* Ill, but not on *both*. If you have four to five ideas filled in on each side of your diagram, this will give you more than enough content to discuss in your answer. Make sure you also spend a moment or two exploring how you will link the various parts.

Writing your response

Once you have planned your content detail and decided on the best order for it, you will need to write using a format such as the following:

1. Introduction: keep it brief and refer to the title; put your title in context.

2. Main body: decide on several short paragraphs and for each one:
   - introduce the point you want to make
   - develop it
   - justify it, giving an example from the novel
   - explain your personal opinion
   - refer back to the question to show it is relevant.

3. Conclusion: no new points; personal reaction; sum up your final position.

Introduction

In the introductory paragraph or sentence, you may wish to briefly place the cultural work that you are studying in context, in a way which is relevant to the question being asked. So, for a question which was asking you to focus on consumerism, you might write:

> Friedrich Dürrenmatt schildert in seinem tragikomischen Theaterstück „Der Besuch der alten Dame", das 1956 zum ersten Mal aufgeführt wurde, die Wirkung des Konsumzeitalters auf die Menschheit.

You may wish to lead into the exam question, by stating what you intend to do in the essay:

> In diesem Aufsatz werde ich analysieren, was der Dramatiker uns über Konsum, Konsumverhalten und die damit verbundenen Probleme sagen möchte.

Main body

Once you are sure about how you are going to structure your answer, aim to deliver a series of clear points which are supported by examples or quotations from the play. For example:

> Im Theaterstück ist das Konsumverhalten der Güllener ein zentrales Thema: Es lässt sich nicht bestreiten, dass Geld oder der Mangel an Geld das Leben der Figuren definiert. Das wird zum Beispiel am Ende des Stücks deutlich, als der Chor den Wohlstand feiert, während die Armut diffamiert wird: ‚Doch nichts ist ungeheurer als die Armut.' Dürrenmatt schlägt mit Ironie vor, dass der Mensch nichts fürchten muss, wenn er nur materiell gut versorgt ist.

— Demonstrates wider thematic knowledge
— Specific point
— Close reference to the play for evidence
— Explanation

Ensure that each part of the question that you answer forms a new paragraph, so that an examiner can follow your train of thought. If you refer to a series of key scenes, then use phrases such as:

Die erste Szene zeigt uns … (*The first scene shows (us) …*)

Am Ende des ersten Akts des Theaterstücks, als Claire die Bedingungen ihres Angebots offenbart … (*At the end of the first act of the play, when Claire reveals the terms of her offer …*)

Gegen Ende des zweiten Akts … (*Towards the end of the second act …*)

Eine wichtige Schlüsselszene im Stück ist …/findet man in … (*An important key scene in the play is/can be found in …*)

Conclusion

A brief conclusion to an essay should offer a clear, personal opinion or summary of the analysis, and it should avoid making any new points. The main body of the essay will have examined various aspects of the play, and at the end you are drawing your own, final summary.

Grammar and vocabulary for your essay

Don't forget that grammar and vocabulary are important for a successful essay, and you will need to demonstrate that you are able to manipulate complex language accurately throughout your writing. Make sure that you prepare for this by:

- **collecting useful language**
- ✓ highlight phrases from this section that you particularly like and learn them
- ✓ learn vocabulary in the various vocabulary boxes and end-of-chapter lists
- ✓ learn key phrases
- **using a variety of structures, such as:**
- ✓ subordinate clauses
- ✓ relative clauses
- ✓ indirect speech
- ✓ word order change to change emphasis
- ✓ indirect questions ('Die Zuschauer wissen noch nicht, warum Claire Zachanassian ihr bizarres Gefolge mitbringt.')
- ✓ comparatives and superlatives
- ✓ the subjunctive
- ✓ the passive
- ✓ rhetorical questions
- **reading more widely:**
- ✓ track down some research or articles on *Der Besuch der alten Dame*
- ✓ read exam exemplar material
- ✓ select some expressions that you like and can learn easily

Exam answer 'do's and 'don't's

Don't retell the plot of the novel. Identify the key arguments that you want to make in your plan.

Don't go off-topic. Stay focused on the question, keep rereading it as you write. Make a plan and stick to it.

Don't make a series of unsupported assertions. Always use evidence from the text to underpin your ideas, whether it's an example or a quotation.

Avoid repetitions: this is a waste of time and words. Good planning will help you avoid this. Number the points in your plan and tick them off as you write.

Don't just reproduce a pre-planned essay. Always answer the exact question in the exam, rather than trying to recall a related question which you prepared at home or in class.

Don't underestimate the power of planning. Many potential pitfalls can be rectified at planning stage. Make sure that you make time for this.

Don't lose track of time! When preparing for a written exam, time yourself. You will need time to plan. Make sure you leave time for proofreading too.

Achieving the best marks

Ensure that you know the requirements for achieving the best marks. These will include the following points:

✓ Analyse an issue, theme or the cultural/social context *critically.*

✓ Use *convincing* interpretations and arguments.

✓ *Justify* your arguments by referring to *evidence* from *Der Besuch der alten Dame*

✓ Arguments and conclusions must be *detailed, logical and well-linked.*

✓ All your responses should be *relevant* to the question.

✓ Use consistently *varied grammatical structures.*

✓ Use consistently *varied vocabulary,* including appropriate terminology for analysing a play.

✓ Ensure a high level of *accuracy.* Any errors must not hinder comprehension of your arguments.

✓ Demonstrate an *accurate manipulation* of language.

Useful phrases

Die ganz zentrale Frage des Theaterstücks ist für mich … The most central question of the play for me is …

Ein wichtiges/weiteres Beispiel in diesem Zusammenhang ist … An important/further example in this context is …

Es muss erwähnt werden, dass … It must be mentioned that …

Dies zeigt sich auf verschiedene Weisen. This demonstrates itself in various ways.

Zusammenfassend könnte man sagen, dass … To sum up, one could say that …

Es stellt sich die Frage … The question has to be asked …

Es scheint also, dass … It seems then that …

Es lässt sich daraus schließen, dass … It can be concluded then that …

Wenn man die Ausgangsfrage betrachtet, … When one considers the starting question …

Meines Erachtens/Meinem Erachten nach … In my view …

Ich könnte mir vorstellen, dass … I could imagine that …

Ich akzeptiere, dass … I accept that …

Ich bezweifle, dass … I doubt that …

Ich bin überzeugt, dass … I am convinced that …

In gleicher Weise … In a similar way …

Außerdem/Darüber hinaus … Moreover/Furthermore …

Im Gegensatz dazu … By contrast …

Sample questions

AS

1

Erklären Sie, inwiefern sich Alfred Ill im Laufe der Tragikomödie *Der Besuch der alten Dame* verändert. Sie können die folgenden Stichpunkte verwenden:

- **Ill als zukünftiger Bürgermeister und Hoffungsträger für Güllen**
- **Ill und seine Vergangenheit**
- **Ill bekommt Angst, sucht Hilfe und versucht zu fliehen**
- **Bedeutung seiner Erkenntnis und seiner Ermordung.**

2

Welche Bedeutung haben Symbole im Theaterstück Der Besuch der alten Dame?
Wie reagieren Sie auf diese Symbole? Sie können die folgenden Stichpunkte
verwenden:

• die Farben Gelb und Schwarz

• Vergleich zwischen dem Panther und Ill

• die Beziehung der Eunuchen zu Ill und Claire

• Ihre Meinung zu diesen Symbolen.

3

Welche Rolle spielt das Thema ‚Materialismus' im Theaterstück Der Besuch der
alten Dame? Berücksichtigen Sie in Ihrer Antwort die folgenden Punkte:

• Zeichen von Armut

• Zeichen des steigenden Wohlstands

• Abhängigkeit von Konsumwaren

• Ill als Retter des materiellen Aufstiegs.

A Level

1

‚Werte und Ideale haben keinen Platz in der heutigen Gesellschaft.' Beurteilen Sie,
wie weit diese Aussage auf das Theaterstück Der Besuch der alten Dame zutrifft.

2

Vergleichen Sie die beiden Hauptfiguren dieses Theaterstücks. Sind beide Helden?
Analysieren Sie diese Frage.

3

Welche sprachlichen, nichtsprachlichen und dramatischen Mittel verwendet Dürrenmatt, die das Theaterstück Der Besuch der alten Dame zu einer Tragikomödie
machen?

4

Untersuchen Sie, warum die Charaktere in diesem Theaterstück Gerechtigkeit
suchen. Inwiefern sind sie dabei erfolgreich?

Sample answers

AS sample answer 1

> **Untersuchen Sie, inwiefern das Sprichwort ‚Geld allein macht nicht glücklich' auf Claire Zachanassian zutrifft. Diese Stichpunkte können verwendet werden:**
> - **Vergleich mit Claires Vergangenheit und ihr ererbter Reichtum**
> - **Was Claire sich mit Geld alles kaufen kann**
> - **Claires Angebot**
> - **Claires Rache und Erfüllung ihres Traums.**

Geld und Reichtum sind eines der zentralen Themen in Dürrenmatts Theaterstück „Der Besuch der alten Dame". Claire Zachanassian, die alte Dame, ist Milliardärin und hat sichtlich genug Geld und viel Besitz. Es stellt sich allerdings die Frage, ob sie wirklich glücklich ist.

Im Laufe des Theaterstücks erfahren wir von Claires Vergangenheit. Als junges, eher armes Mädchen hatte sie viel Spaß und spielte den Güllenern den einen oder anderen Streich, zum Beispiel, wenn sie den Männern auf die Köpfe spuckte. Auch während der Beziehung mit Ill schien Claire glücklich gewesen zu sein. Dieses Glück endete jedoch, als zwei Männer eine falsche Zeugenaussage machten. Als unglückliche, vertriebene Mutter landete sie in einem Hamburger Bordell. Doch die Milliarden ihres ersten Ehemanns Zachanassian machten sie nach seinem Tod zu einer reichen Frau.

Von Anfang an wissen wir, dass Claire Zachanassians Geld den Güllenern aus ihrer Armut und ihrer Trostlosigkeit helfen soll. Allerdings erfahren wir erst viel später, dass die Armut der Güllener von Claire geplant war, sogar der Konradsweilerwald, wo sich Ill und Claire liebten, war von Claire gekauft worden. Claire hatte nämlich alles in Güllen gekauft und ruiniert. Als Grund gibt sie an, dass sie Gerechtigkeit für ein vergangenes Verbrechen möchte. Sie ist reich geworden, obwohl das Verbrechen sie unglücklich gemacht hat. Sie hat die Güllener meiner Meinung nach jedoch nicht nur unglücklich, sondern auch arm gemacht. Dies belegen auch die vier Güllener im ersten Akt, wenn sie meinen, dass Güllen und die Güllener ‚ruiniert' seien.

Nicht um die Güllener aus ihrer Armut zu führen, sondern um Rache an Ill zu üben, unterbreitet Claire Zachanassian das Angebot. Zumindest glauben das anfangs die Güllener und wir Zuschauer. Es wird aber später klar, dass Claire trotz ihres Gelds und ihrer vielen Ehemänner nie wirklich glücklich geworden ist. Sie hält an dem ‚Traum von Leben, von Liebe, von Vertrauen' fest. Das Angebot der Milliarde sowie Ills Tod helfen ihr,

Good introduction; informs reader about key themes.

Useful word to show level of analysis, but not clear which part of the play this refers to.

Concrete example given; could have been slightly more precise but illustrates the point made.

Excellent phrase to link the points about her happiness and unhappiness.

This sentence summarises well how Claire got to her wealth.

An important aspect of the play; good complex structure.

Valid point but a bit of a jump from one point to the next.

The focus has to be on Claire, as opposed to the 'Güllener'.

Successful link to previous paragraph.

Good attempt at analysis; relevant to the essay task.

dieses Ziel zu erreichen.

Successful conclusion; refers back to essay question and states personal opinion.

Meines Erachtens ist es mit Claires Abreise und der Errichtung des Mausoleums für Ill ersichtlich, dass Claire am Ende des Stücks glücklicher ist. Daher bin ich überzeugt, dass das Sprichwort auf Claire zutrifft: obwohl Geld allein nicht glücklich macht, erreicht Claire ihr erträumtes Glück durch ihre Milliarde, die die Güllener so nötig haben.

Commentary

Overall, a successful answer which is well structured and uses a mixture of complex and simple phrases, which influence the flow of text positively. Throughout, the answer focuses on the essay themes and successfully unpicks the proverb. At one point the focus is lost when talking about the people of Güllen and their happiness rather than about Claire Zachanassian, but the answer ends with a strong conclusion.

AS sample answer 2

Wie reagieren Sie auf die Beschreibung der Bürger von Güllen? Warum? Benutzen Sie die folgenden Stichpunkte:

- **die Reaktion nach dem Angebot**
- **die Veränderung der Güllener**
- **die Güllener als Freunde**
- **die Güllener als Mörder.**

Useful positioning of the citizens of Güllen as minor characters.

Good summary of their function in the play.

Useful plot summary with two very relevant quotations.

'verändern': good attempt to analyse the characters by referring back to the play.

For whom?

Im Theaterstück „Der Besuch der alten Dame" spielen die Güllener eine wichtige Rolle, obwohl sie nur Nebenfiguren sind. Sie sind es, die Ill im Stich lassen und ihn töten, um ihren Wohlstand zu behalten.

Das großzügige Angebot der Milliardärin Claire Zachanassian wird vom Bürgermeister ‚im Namen der Stadt Güllen' abgelehnt, weil es den Tod Ills verlangt. Obwohl die Güllener am Anfang des zweiten Akts mit ihren Aussagen hinter Ill stehen, kaufen sie viele neue und teuere Produkte. Da sie kein Geld haben, kaufen sie auf Kredit. ‚Schreiben's auf' ist eine ständig wiederholte Phrase und die Güllener stürzen sich immer mehr in Schulden.

Der wachsende Wohlstand verändert die Bürger, die anfangs nicht nur Freunde von Ill waren, sondern ihn sogar zum nächsten Bürgermeister machen wollten. Doch dann wird Ill zum Hindernis. Das wird vor allem deutlich, als die Journalisten nach Claires Hochzeit in der Stadt sind und einige Güllener Angst haben, dass Ill die Wahrheit erzählen könnte. Wenn die Wahrheit in die Zeitungen kommt, dann kann das das Ende des neuen, genussvollen Lebens sein. Genau dieses Leben wollen die Bürger von Güllen behalten und es macht sie zu Mördern. Für mich ist es sehr enttäuschend zu sehen, dass auch der Pfarrer und der Lehrer an dieser Mordtat beteiligt sind und dass der Doktor mit dem Ausruf ‚Herzschlag' sich selbst, die Bürger und die Welt anlügt.

Zusammenfassend könnte man sagen, dass die Bürger von Güllen ihren Ill geopfert haben, um selbst im Wohlstand und Reichtum zu leben. Zugleich sind sie aber auch ein wichtiges Werkzeug der alten Dame: die Güllener machten sich die Hände schmutzig und nicht Claire selbst.

Which truth is referred to here?

Good attempt at interpretation.

Effective introduction of personal opinion.

Relevant, but doesn't reflect a reaction as required by the task.

Effective conclusion.

Commentary

A successful attempt at answering this question. All bullet points have been covered, the various paragraphs have been interlinked well, and there is a logical flow of argument. The aspect of 'reaction' to the citizens of Güllen could have been strengthened. Having said this, the powerful conclusion could be interpreted as a personal reaction to the play. Good use of brief quotations.

A Level sample answer 1

> Im letzten Gespräch mit Ill erklärt die alte Dame: ‚Ich will [meinen Traum] wieder errichten mit meinen Milliarden, die Vergangenheit ändern, indem ich dich vernichte.' Analysieren Sie Claire Zachanassians Verständnis von Recht und Gerechtigkeit.

Neben Armut, Reichtum und Materialismus sind Recht und Gerechtigkeit zentrale Themen in Dürrenmatts Tragikomödie „Der Besuch der alten Dame". Die betagte Dame will mit ihren Milliarden Gerechtigkeit kaufen. Bereits gegen Ende des ersten Akts wird uns als Zuschauer klar, dass sie von dem überzeugt ist, was sie sagt: ‚Ich kann sie mir leisten. Eine Milliarde für Güllen, wenn jemand Alfred Ill tötet.'

Diese Forderung und ihr Warten auf die Ermordung Ills wurden von Claire genau geplant. Die Schmerzen, die ihr als junges Mädchen zugefügt wurden, will sie nun rächen und die ihr damals untersagte Gerechtigkeit wieder herstellen. Beim Erreichen ihres Ziels hilft ihr natürlich ihr Reichtum,

Informative introduction demonstrates knowledge of key themes.

Summarises the key message of plot well.

Quotation whets reader's appetite.

Clever link to previous paragraph.

Some readers might not be clear which particular pain is being referred to.

Successful attempt at analysis.

Supporting evidence from the plot given.

Good phrase, but what is meant by 'freie Definition'?

Helpful explanation.

Shows an in-depth understanding of the text.

Repetition of 'Schwäche' used successfully to link points.

A further angle on how Claire deals with justice; a well-developed paragraph.

Fairly brief but poignant conclusion; no reference to 'Recht', though.

aber auch ihre Überzeugung, dass Recht und Gerechtigkeit manipulierbar sind. Das wird deutlich, wenn wir erfahren, dass sie das amerikanische Justizsystem umgangen hat und zwei zum Tode verurteilte Gangster freikaufte, um für sie zu arbeiten. Ein weiteres Beispiel ihrer etwas freien Definition von Recht sind die beiden Eunuchen, die gegen sie ausgesagt hatten, als sie ein junges Mädchen war: zur Strafe wurden sie kastriert und geblendet. Selbstverständlich machte sie das nicht eigenhändig, aber für eine gewisse Summe wird sie diese Taten in Auftrag gegeben haben.

Ich verstehe das Angebot und die Bedingung an die Güllener als so einen Auftrag. Die Güllener werden von ihr am Ende des Stücks mit einer Milliarde belohnt. Was sie – außer dem Lehrer – nicht wirklich bemerken, ist, dass die alte Dame wie eine Schicksalsgöttin die Fäden zieht, um sich ihren Traum zu erfüllen. Sie hat als junges Mädchen die Schwäche der Menschen kennengelernt. Diese Schwäche nützt sie aus, um Gerechtigkeit zu erlangen. Die Güllener nehmen ihren Gerechtigkeitssinn als Vorwand, die Milliarde anzunehmen und dafür Ill zu töten. Was die Güllener in ihrer Kaufsucht sichtlich vergessen, ist, dass sie selbst zu Tätern und Schuldigen werden. Als Schuldige haben sie Claire zu ihrer Gerechtigkeit verholfen, haben dabei jedoch ihre eigenen Hände und Seelen schmutzig gemacht.

Deshalb komme ich für mich zu dem Schluss, dass Claires Verständnis von Gerechtigkeit ein sehr persönliches ist. Sie will Gerechtigkeit, um die Ungerechtigkeit vor 45 Jahren zu rächen und ihren ,Traum von Leben, von Liebe, von Vertrauen' zu verwirklichen.

Commentary

Overall, a successful and linguistically sophisticated response. An insightful knowledge of the play is demonstrated, as well as a good understanding of the theme. The focus seems to lie more on 'justice' rather than 'law'. Having said this, a well-structured and coherent argument is developed. At times, the answer assumes that the reader has a thorough knowledge of the play by alluding to certain aspects of the plot rather than explaining them.

A Level sample answer 2

> **Inwiefern trifft die Redewendung ,Die Vergangenheit holt uns immer ein!' auf die verschiedenen Figuren/Charaktere im Theaterstück *Der Besuch der alten Dame* zu?**

Die Redewendung ‚Die Vergangenheit holt uns immer ein!' trifft meines Erachtens auf das Theaterstück „Der Besuch der alten Dame" auf jeden Fall für einige Figuren zu. In meinem Aufsatz möchte ich mich auf die folgenden Charaktere konzentrieren: die Hauptfigur Ill und die beiden schrägen Eunuchen.

Obwohl das Theaterstück in der Gegenwart spielt, gibt es viele Handlungen aus der Vergangenheit, die diese Gegenwart beeinflussen. Eines der wichtigsten Beispiele dafür ist Ills Verhalten gegenüber Klara Wäscher, der heutigen Claire Zachanassian, als beide jung waren. Seine Vaterschaft verleugnete er damals, weil er trotz seiner Liebe zu Claire Mathilde, die Tochter des Krämers, heiratete, um finanziell abgesichert zu sein.

Die Verleugnung ist jedoch nicht das einzige Fehlverhalten, das in Claires Augen Ills Ermordung fordert. Die für Claire wohl verletzendste Handlung war, dass ihr geliebter Ill Jakob Hühnelein und Ludwig Sparr mit Schnaps bezahlt hatte, um eine Falschaussage zu machen. Als reiche Frau lässt sie die beiden blenden und kastrieren. Seine dunkle Vergangenheit holt Ill also auch durch die beiden Diener der Claire Zachanassian ein. Meiner Meinung nach könnte man sie fast als Personifizierung der Redewendung ‚Die Vergangenheit holt uns immer ein!' sehen, denn sie sind es, die gemeinsam mit dem damaligen Richter den Güllenern die Wahrheit über Ill erzählen.

Diese Wahrheit bringt die Güllener dazu, Ill als nicht ehrwürdigen Nachfolger des Bürgermeisters, als Schuft und dann am Schluss sogar als ‚Schwein' zu bezeichnen, was ihnen die Ermordung Ills leichter macht.

Ich denke aber auch, dass die Güllener selbst, die Claire nach dem falschen Gerichtsurteil aus Güllen vertrieben haben und in ihrem Wohlstand weiterlebten, von der Vergangenheit eingeholt wurden. Der finanzielle Ruin der Stadt, die Schließung der verschiedenen Industrien sind nicht nur ein Zeichen des wirtschaftlichen Verfalls, sondern auch eine gewisse Bestrafung für ihr Schweigen und ihr Dulden von Unwahrheiten.

Am Schluss stellt sich für mich die Frage, ob die Güllener nach dem Mord an Ill in ihrer von Konsumgütern gefüllten Zukunft auch einmal von der Vergangenheit eingeholt werden. Wenn ja, dann werden auch sie teuer bezahlen müssen. Bleibt nur zu hoffen, dass sie ihr Verbrechen nicht wie Ill mit ihrem Leben bezahlen müssen.

Margin annotations:
- Effective introduction.
- Introduces focus on the past well.
- Supports argument with a relevant example.
- Not quite accurate: we do not know that he is denying the fatherhood because of a planned marriage to Mathilde.
- Effective link established.
- Attempt at analysis.
- Plot cleverly interwoven with proverb.
- Opinion with good attempt at analysis.
- Supportive justification.
- 'diese' used well to refer back to aspect of previous sentence.
- Analysis demonstrates in-depth knowledge of play.
- A worthwhile argument with good analysis; could have been strengthened by quotation.
- Different but effective opening of concluding statement.
- Useful explanation of previous statement.

Commentary

This is a sophisticated response which demonstrates not only an in-depth knowledge of the play but also a good level of analysis, despite the inaccuracy towards the end of the second paragraph. It is a well-structured submission of high-level German. It is worth noting that the answer does not rely overly on pre-learned sentence openers and uses varied methods, including grammatical devices, extremely well. A particular strength is the way in which the proverb is analysed in line with the task set.

Glossary

anagnorisis *die Anagnorisis* the point, especially in Greek tragedy, when a character comes to a realisation about his or her true identity or situation, or that of another character

Bertolt Brecht an influential German poet, playwright and theatrical reformer whose epic theatre developed drama as a social and ideological forum for left-wing causes

capitalism *der Kapitalismus* an economic system and an ideology based on private ownership of the means of production and their operation for profit

catharsis *die Katharsis* the process of releasing, and thereby providing relief from, strong or repressed emotions

Clotho *Klotho* one of the three Greek goddesses of Fate; she was the spinner who spun the thread of life

collective *die Gemeinschaft/das Kollektiv* people acting as a group

communism *der Kommunismus* a system of social organisation in which all property is owned by the community and each person contributes and receives according to his or her ability and needs

dramatic irony *die dramatische Ironie* a technique by which the full significance of words and actions on stage becomes clear to the audience but not to the character(s)

epic theatre *das epische Theater* the style and techniques developed by Bertolt Brecht, used to allow an audience to maintain an emotional objectivity necessary to learn the truth about their society

Federal Republic of Germany *die Bundesrepublik Deutschland/BRD* in May 1949, as a result of mounting tensions between the Soviets and the Allied occupiers of Germany, the Federal Republic of Germany ('West Germany') was formally established as an independent nation

foreshadowing *die Vorahnung* a warning or suggestion of a future event

Freytag's Pyramid *Freytags Pyramide* the five-stage structure of a drama illustrated by Gustav Freytag in 1863

German Democratic Republic *die Deutsche Demokratische Republik/DDR* 'East Germany' was established in 1949 from the area of Germany that was occupied by the Soviet Union

German Mark *die Deutsche Mark* the 'Deutsche Mark' ('DM') replaced the 'Reichsmark' and remained West Germany's official currency until it was replaced by the Euro

harbinger *der Vorbote* a herald or forewarning

the Holocaust *der Holocaust* the period of persecution and extermination of European Jews by Nazi Germany

humanism *der Humanismus* a non-religious belief system which uses reason and ethics to inform decisions about human welfare and how best to live

ironic *ironisch* meaning the opposite of what you actually say

Lais *Lais von Korinth* a prostitute from Greek Mythology

Marxist *marxistisch* following the political and economic philosophy of Karl Marx and Friedrich Engels which forms the basis of communism; a central Marxist idea is that of class struggle, through which oppression of the working classes should be overcome to create a classless society

Medea *Medea* a character from Greek mythology; in the play *Medea* by Euripides, Medea's husband Jason leaves her for another woman; she consequently kills the children she had had with Jason

NATO *die NATO* the North Atlantic Treaty Organisation was created in 1949, to represent a military deterrent against the Soviet Union

occcupied zones *die Besatzungszonen* at the end of the Second World War, Britain, the US, France and the Soviet Union divided Germany into four occupation zones between 1945 and 1952; the purpose was to assist Germany in its rebuilding but also to control Germany

Parca *die Parze* female personification of destiny in ancient Roman religion and myth; the Romans identified the Parcae with the three Greek 'Fates'

Passion Plays *die Passionsspiele* plays performed at Easter depicting the trial, suffering and death of Jesus Christ

reparations *die Entschädigungen/ Reparationen* compensation for war damage paid by a defeated state

rhetoric *die Rhetorik* language designed to have a persuasive or impressive effect

satire *die Satire* criticising the vices or stupidity of others through humour, ridicule, exaggeration or irony

Third Reich *das Dritte Reich* the period of German history when Adolf Hitler was in power, 1933–1945

Answers

Plot and Structure

Aufgabe 2 *(page 10)*

1. She seems like a Parca (Fate) to me.

2. Claire could be a Goddess of Fate.

3. One should rename her.

4. The teacher deems her capable of spinning life's threads.

Aufgabe 5 *(page 14)*

a. 1. du kannst nicht fordern (Das kannst du doch nicht fordern!), **2.** Das Leben ging weiter, **3.** dein Verrat (deinen Verrat), **4.** daß wir abrechnen, **5.** die Zeit aufheben (daß die Zeit aufgehoben würde)

Aufgabe 16 *(page 23)*

a. F, **b.** F, **c.** N, **d.** R, **e.** F

Context

Aufgabe 1 *(page 38)*

a. deren, **b.** der, **c.** das, **d.** die (pl), **e.** die

Aufgabe 6 *(page 48)*

a. 1. h, **2.** f, **3.** g, **4.** b, **5.** d, **6.** a, **7.** c, **8.** e

Language

Aufgabe 3 *(page 72)*

a. Verdoppelung, **b.** Vorahnungen, **c.** kollektiver Satzbau, **d.** singsanghafte Wiederholung, **e.** Satzdekonstruierung

Themes

Aufgabe 1 *(page 83)*

Einige Symbole sind: Kirchenglocke; der goldene Zahn; der Plan für ein neues Rathaus; die gelben Schuhe; der neue Wagen von Karl.

Aufgabe 8 *(page 93)*

a. F, **b.** R, **c.** F, **d.** F

OXFORD
UNIVERSITY PRESS

Great Clarendon Street, Oxford, OX2 6DP, United Kingdom

Oxford University Press is a department of the University of Oxford. It furthers the University's objective of excellence in research, scholarship, and education by publishing worldwide. Oxford is a registered trade mark of Oxford University Press in the UK and in certain other countries.

British Library Cataloguing in Publication Data

Data available

ISBN 978-0-19-841839-9

Kindle edition ISBN 978-0-19-841832-0

3 5 7 9 10 8 6 4

Printed and bound by CPI Group (UK) Ltd., Croydon CR0 4YY

Acknowledgements
The publisher and author would like to thank the following for permission to use photographs and other copyright material:

Extracts from: Friedrich Dürrenmatt, *Der Besuch der alten Dame*, Copyright © 1986 Diogenes Verlag AG Zurich, Switzerland. All rights reserved.

Scripture quotations [marked NIV] taken from the Holy Bible, New International Version Anglicised Copyright © 1979, 1984, 2011 Biblica. Used by permission of Hodder & Stoughton Ltd, an Hachette UK company. All rights reserved.

p.43: Friedrich Dürrenmatt, *Theater: Essays, Gedichte, Reden*, Copyright © 1986 Diogenes Verlag AG Zurich, Switzerland. All rights reserved.

p.89: Eberhard Falcke, *Friedrich Dürrenmatt: "Der Besuch der alten Dame"*, aus der Reihe: Klassiker der Schullektüre (3/3), SWR2 Wissen. Reproduced with permission from Dr Eberhard Falcke.

Every effort has been made to contact copyright holders of material reproduced in this book. Any omissions will be rectified in subsequent printings if notice is given to the publisher.